THE ROAD TO PROSPERITY

THE ROAD TO PROSPERITY

Wealth: How to get it, Keep it, and Profit from it

Al Jacobs

DANA PUBLISHING
P. O. BOX 3143
DANA POINT, CA 92629

THE ROAD TO PROSPERITY

Wealth: How to Get it, Keep it, and Profit from it

By Al Jacobs

Published by:

DANA PUBLISHING

P.O. Box 3143

Dana Point, CA 92629

Library of Congress Cataloging-in-Publication Data

Jacobs, Al

THE ROAD TO PROSPERITY: Wealth: How to Get it,
Keep it, and Profit from it / by Al Jacobs

p. cm.

ISBN 978-0-9860500-0-8

X1. Finance, Personal   I. Title

HG179.L69 2014 332.024 01

Library of Congress Control Number: 2013952474

Cover design by Mirt Norgren, MN Designs, Mission Viejo, CA
Edited by Geoff and Joan Davies, Seal Beach, CA
Book production coordinated by Ernie Hernandez, Frontline
Publications, Lake Forest, CA

Disclaimer

The purpose of this book is to educate and entertain. The author and Dana Publishing shall have neither liability nor responsibility to any person or entity with respect to any loss or damage caused, or alleged to have been caused, directly or indirectly, by the information contained in this book.

Printed in the United States of America

ACKNOWLEDGMENTS

My personal thanks to . . .

Mirt Norgren, operating as Mirt Norgren Graphic Design, Capistrano Beach, CA, whose artistic and graphic design abilities created the cover of this book. For those of you in need of Mirt's excellent services she can be reached at www.mirt.co.

Geoff and Joan Davies of Seal Beach, CA, my friends of many years, who took the time and trouble to thoroughly edit each page of my manuscript before it became etched in stone. But for their efforts, you would have tripped uncomfortably over my grotesque misspellings and faulty syntax.

Ernie Hernandez, operating as Frontline Publications, Lake Forest, CA, whose computer savvy enabled me to assemble this book in the form you see, and whose Internet abilities are responsible for its reaching a wide audience. Ernie can be reached at www.erniehernandez.us.

My wife, Rene, whose sense of proportion encouraged me, over this past half-century, to delete or condense many of my ramblings for the immense benefit of the readers.

CONTENTS

Preface   i

Chapter 1   1
How to Spend Your Money

Chapter 2   5
How to Avoid Misfortune

Chapter 3   9
Chasing Exotic Investments

Chapter 4   13
Marital Wellness: A View from the Ledger

Chapter 5   19
The Cash Value of Honesty

Chapter 6   23
Education: The Bottom Line

Chapter 7   31
Investment American Style

Chapter 8   39
Holding Your Own Against the Establishment

Chapter 9   43
Survival in Tough Times: Smart Shopping

Chapter 10   47
The Seven Fundamentals of Sound Investment

Chapter 11   55
The Economics of a Habit

Chapter 12   61
Panic Time: Problems that Spell Trouble
Chapter 13   65
Tips for the Aspiring Homeowner
Chapter 14   69
How to Instill Responsibility in Your Offspring
Chapter 15   73
Twenty-first Century Thrift and Banking
Chapter 16   77
Random Thoughts on the Road to Prosperity
Chapter 17   85
Second Thought on Investing
Chapter 18   89
Thar's Gold in Them Thar Bonds
Chapter 19   95
Marketing in America: How did it Come to This?
Chapter 20   99
Is Social Security a Gigantic Ponzi Scheme?
Chapter 21   109
Investing like a Millionaire
Chapter 22   113
Peddling Gold: Flimflam at its Finest
Chapter 23   121
Justice Denied
Chapter 24   125
The World of the IPO
Chapter 25   131
Chasing Foreclosures: An Exercise in Fortitude

Chapter 26 137
 College you can Afford

Chapter 27 145
 Roth IRA Conversions: It's in the Numbers

Chapter 28 151
 How to Dispose of an Unwanted Partner

Chapter 29 155
 A Cure for Alzheimer's Disease?

Chapter 30 163
 A Thimbleful of Prosperity

Chapter 31 169
 Proceed at your own Risk

Chapter 32 175
 Money and Health—the Inseparable Link

Chapter 33 183
 An Investment Lesson

Chapter 34 189
 "Sit Still and Behave Yourself!"

Chapter 35 193
 Where Charity Begins

Chapter 36 199
 How to Cope with the Increased Cost of Dying

Chapter 37 203
 Five Frivolous Items that are Really Worth it

Chapter 38 207
 25 Signs Showing you Can Handle Money

Chapter 39 211
 A View from the Far Side

PREFACE

Your stature is measured by
the way you handle success.

Every book written has two purposes: stated and actual. How refreshing if both are the same, but that asks for too much.

Browsing through purported non-fiction is illuminating. The works normally fall into one of three categories: a desire to educate, a revelation of truth, or a call to action.

Do you recall the 1980s book of the adopted daughter of a well-known deceased actress, depicting her claims of parental abuse? During the promotion tour on the media circuit, she maintained as her intent not to profit from a brutally disparaged reputation but, rather, to shed light on the grim subject of child abuse. With such a high-minded goal, it sold well. At about the same time, the son of a famous singer and actor promoted a book similarly critical of his own late father. When asked bluntly by a Los Angeles radio talk show host why he chose to defame his father, he calmly and frankly replied, "I can use the money."

An author's desire to profit is a strong inducement. This is legitimate—even laudable—though such honesty is rare. Despite intense negotiations with agents and publishers over every financial consequence, the details dare not be revealed. Admitting to a profit motive seems to demean both author and book. The unwritten law: Never admit being in it for the money.

There's a second justification for authorship even more compelling than profit. It's the ego satisfaction from seeing your words in print for the world to admire. Many a wealthy notable, judging from the proliferation of such works, appears in print for no other reason than desire for even greater notoriety. Whether actually written by the author or simply "ghosted," the publication serves the purpose. Still, the market remains thin. Hardback copies can be found littering bargain bins a year after the first and only printing, at clearance prices less than two dollars. If you scan some of them, you understand better the term "vast wasteland." The only point many achieve is to demonstrate that making a public fool of oneself is an occupational hazard of being a celebrity.

While far too many of these books are clearly an embarrassment, a few are worthwhile. An author who scarcely needed the money or notoriety wrote one of the finer examples. *How to Be Rich*, by the late J. Paul Getty, is far more than the usual collection of get-rich-quick nostrums filling the shelves of bookstores. In it, Getty gave sound advice to would-be executives on the importance of character traits as well as practical suggestions on effective business practices. In addition, he stressed the responsibilities that go with wealth and success. Though it deserves to be required reading in every school of business, it remains mostly unknown and, unfortunately, unread.

This brings us to the purpose of this book. My aim is to encourage the readers to develop those talents needed to become financially successful and to conduct themselves in ways to stay successful. I firmly believe prosperity is attainable by most people, if only they will adhere to certain sensible life habits. The pages which follow describe these habits, with examples of what happens when things are done right . . . and also when things are done wrong.

You're now entitled to ask: What brings financial success? Why do some persons rise to the pinnacle while others, who seem equally deserving, wallow in mediocrity? Still vivid in my memory is a line from the 1969 movie, *Goodbye, Columbus*, featuring that venerable actor Jack Klugman, who portrayed a crude and overbearing, but wealthy, plumbing contractor. In one scene during a family party, his cousin, a disgruntled college teacher, in referring to Klugman, blurts out: "I don't understand it. I've got more brains in my little finger than he's got in his whole body. Why is he at the top and I'm at the bottom?" Perhaps it's natural to equate intelligence with financial success, and one of the more overused put-downs is the perennial question: "If you're so smart, how come you're not rich?" The fact is, however, affluence is not confined to the brilliant, nor are the brightest people necessarily the most prosperous. As a case in point, many members of the international high-IQ organization, *Mensa*, are of modest means. This is not meant as an endorsement of stupidity, for most certainly dimwittedness does little to promote wealth accumulation. Nonetheless, high intelligence is not the answer, and Robert Heller in his 1974 book *The Common Millionaire* points out that, down through the ages, a lot of untalented people managed to make a million dollars.

Possibly high intelligence actually acts as a bar to financial prosperity. Unlike success in scientific endeavors, which requires profound skills to solve often complex problems, the routine applications commonly demanded in wealth accumulation is one requiring little but a repetition of procedures, with no continual input of brainpower needed. Quite likely a mind capable of absorbing and processing new and stimulating information finds these demands a monotonous exercise offering little satisfaction—except for the obvious benefits of having wealth. If this is so, the link between intelligence and financial success is not the direct correlation we might expect, and beyond some level, increased intellect is actually a *deterrent* in the wealth-generating process? In this connection, I've long suspected financial success is enhanced as the intelligence quotient reaches an optimum of about 115, thereafter declining as IQ increases. If this is the case, we of questionable intellect may take heart; there surely is a fortune waiting for us.

So the question remains: Exactly what qualities are most helpful in acquiring and retaining wealth? From my observations it appears the necessary ingredients include habits of thrift and moderation, the diligent pursuance of a plan of action, and just plain good luck. Admittedly the second of these requires some aptitude, which eliminates the truly inept from the game. But on the whole the meld of these character traits seems to determine the outcome. And it's my belief "diligence" is by far the most important of these characteristics. I don't suppose I need explain diligence other than say you simply keep plugging away at a project until you finish it. Winners do this; losers don't.

There's a fourth characteristic, not planted so firmly in the psyche, which can be learned. The quality is *discernment*, most accurately defined as the ability to distinguish illusion from reality. It's this capability, to a great extent attitudinal, that's the hallmark of the skeptic, and through practice and repetition it can become an established thought process. Thus, when on the 10 o'clock television news, a DEA official proclaims "another major victory" in the federal government's War on Drugs, while displaying agents posing beside a record cache of narcotics, do you instinctively question the sort of victory won? And for those of you old enough to remember the 1990s, when President Clinton announced the dispatch of American troops to the Yugoslav province of Bosnia in late 1995 to help facilitate the Dayton accord, with an assurance of their withdrawal within one year, did you mentally add 365 days to determine whether the date fell *before* or *after* the scheduled presidential election? And did it not surprise you, following Mr. Clinton's 1996 reelection, the term of the occupation force continued to be extended? In addition, did you somehow anticipate that in 2001, newly elected President Bush would declare the U.S. presence in the Balkans to be essential? Are you not surprised that in 2013, our army's 38th Cavalry Regiment stationed in Kosovo was involved in removing barricades mounted by Serbs so to facilitate access to an area north of Kosovo? And finally, do you suspect, barring some catastrophe, U.S. troops will still be there on New Year's Day in the year 2025? If your answer to all these questions is "yes," you're well on your way to *discernment* and true understanding.

I mentioned the term *skeptic*; this deserves some elaboration. When you hear the word, what comes to mind? Do you imagine creationism ridiculed? Perhaps you reflect on a television interview debating Elvis Presley's recent sighting in a Memphis restaurant. Possibly the term describes you, laughing at the promises by the presidential candidates to lower taxes? Whatever your view, the picture is often one of curled lip and perpetual sneer—of a smirker rejecting anything and everything.

In essence, a skeptic is someone not easily persuaded, suspending judgment while collecting and weighing evidence. Skepticism, the questioning of accepted wisdom, does not deserve its bad rap. Around for a long time, the names associated with it include the likes of Galileo, David Hume, Imanuel Kant, Herbert Spencer, and George Santayana, to mention just a few. Over the centuries these and many lesser-knowns pursued their fields, employing objectivity in the quest for knowledge. Most of these men found it an arduous trip, as the tide rarely favors those who question conventional beliefs.

To this day skepticism is viewed unfavorably by society, even among those who consider themselves enlightened. One reason is the public's blurring of the line between the questioning approach of the *skeptic* and the dismissive attitude of the *cynic*. Admittedly the doctrine of Cynicism as a philosophy dates back to the fourth century B.C. and to its founder, Diogenes, best remembered as the lampbearer in search of the elusive honest man. However, it never became an important school of thought, with cynics throughout history recognized more by their nonconformity and eccentricity than the force of their logic. Today cynicism is perceived as little more than a distrust of human nature and motives. Nonetheless, there are resemblances between skepticism and cynicism which cannot be shaken.

Irrespective of the similarities, there's a fundamental difference. It is the recognition of one of life's more helpful rules of thumb:

Ninety-five percent of everything is nonsense.

The cynic dismisses everything as nonsense; the skeptic recognizes that some portion may be valid and seeks to find it.

There's a common admonition: Believe nothing you hear and only half of what you see. This is adequate for the cynic but not the skeptic. Just as a stopped clock is right twice a day, part of what you hear is possibly believable and shouldn't be dismissed out of hand. Conversely, far less than half of what you see, or *think* you see, may be valid and dare not be accepted on faith. And even if half of something is believable, the trick is to figure out which half. This is where skepticism, not cynicism, applies. Being right by accident doesn't help much. You must know *why* you're right.

So much for skepticism's development, where it fits into the world, and how it differs from its chief rival. Its principles apply to every human endeavor and deserve consideration in the situations you confront. As no two persons bring with them the same experiences, their sets of conclusions on an observation will not necessarily match. But what *should* match is a questioning approach and an unwillingness either to believe or disbelieve without persuasive evidence.

Let me sum up the subject of skepticism with the following thought. If, as I contend, ninety-five percent of everything is nonsense, then it suggests you'll do well to restrict your life, as best you're able, to the other five percent. In practice this means you seek to avoid the world's nonsense. And how do you do this specifically? In all sorts of ways. You don't buy lottery tickets, designed to fleece you. You don't breathe into your lungs the smoke from cigarettes, designed to kill you. You don't make monetary contributions to fraudulent organizations, designed to steal from you while they insult you. There are countless other examples, which you'll learn as you read the chapters of this book.

I want to convey another message before you begin to wade into the many topics presented in this book. The thoughts and suggestions presented here are only partly mine. I've borrowed many from others and inserted them at the appropriate places in the text to convey a point or an example. In addition, I admit much of what I've learned over the decades came not the result of shrewd and calculating introspection, but rather revelations which, in many cases, were pounded into me involuntarily. It's pretty well acknowledged in military circles that a recruit can learn a lot of valuable things simply being kicked around the parade grounds for awhile. Let me assure you, I've put in a lot of hours being similarly kicked around and learned many of the lessons well. I hope I can pass them on effectively.

I'll add a final comment. Perhaps this book will be revised and reissued. I'd appreciate input from the reader. Am I off base on some of my views? Do many of my beliefs meet with approval? Where might my conclusions need rethinking? This sort of feedback can be helpful. In this regard, let me extend an invitation: Feel free to forward any comments to me. Be assured they will be read.

1

HOW TO SPEND
YOUR MONEY

The wise use of money is the only
advantage to having it.
Ben Franklin

In an earlier time, under the influence of the traditional *Christian ethic*, virtue assumed a divine quality. Among these principles was thrift, honored for its own sake. I recall a popular tale about the wife of a man of extremely modest means whose food shopping consisted of selecting the lowest priced items from numerous markets. Naturally she walked from store to store—or perhaps "trudged," to add a touch of pathos. In any event, the story served its purpose. It illustrated a frugality next to godliness, with no limit to the exaltation experienced in such behavior.

Things are no longer as they were. A recent report reveals over half a group surveyed refuses to pick up a penny on the ground. Speaking for myself, I'll never pass one by. Perhaps it relates to my recollections as a teen-aged bowling alley pin setter earning a dime a line. A penny represents resetting of ten wooden pins and returning two 16-pound balls. To this day one cent signifies a reward for services rendered. Are my experiences unique? It's hard to say whether this attitude is generational or personal. Regardless, there's more to the wise use of money than mere bargain hunting. A personal consideration transcends the ordinary analysis of value—I call it *marginal benefits of economy*. Let me explain.

There's a term taught in first year Economics known as *marginal utility of money*. The principle is easily illustrated. Consider the case of Bea Reft, annual salary $30,000, who receives a $5,000 increase. Her life is measurably improved. She can now eat out a little more often, join the neighborhood health club and buy that pair of unaffordable black Amalfi pumps. Contrast this with Greta Gotrocks, earning $180,000 per year, who likewise receives a $5,000 pay increase. Compared with her standard of living before, that relatively small additional amount is meaningless. The likelihood is Greta will never notice the difference.

In concept, *marginal benefits of economy* is akin to *marginal utility of money* wherein the perceived benefit from an expenditure relates to financial status. Several factors, foremost among them cash flow and net worth, interact to determine the relative value of parsimony. The more prosperous a person becomes, the less meaningful the benefit from a cost-conscious economic decision. If the 9-month old car radio of Elizabeth F. Rugle, a housekeeper earning $500 per week, malfunctions, she should invoke her warranty despite the fact she must do without for the four weeks it will take for the radio to be reinstalled. However, if the same misfortune befalls Edward P. Rosperous, a $210,000 per year title company executive, he may ignore the warranty, buy a new car radio for $200 and install it at once. The pleasure of listening to the radio for those four weeks provides a greater marginal benefit to him than the price he pays. Similarly, at the extreme, Michael Bloomberg was fully justified in spending sixty million dollars for the pleasure, as mayor of New York, of telling citizens they may not enjoy a soft drink of more than sixteen ounces. There is probably no way he might have spent discretionary dollars more enjoyably.

Finally, consider another principle running counter to our marginal benefits principle: *diminishing returns*. Although the actual law of diminishing returns formulated in the eighteenth century pertained to a relationship between input and output of productive resources, the concept can be expanded to relate to an individual's personal expenditures. As an illustration, a pair of stereo speakers faithfully reproducing sound over the frequency range 30 to 16,000 hertz (cycles per second) costs $250. By employing the ultimate in design and manufacturing techniques, this expands to the range of the human ear, 20 to 20,000 hertz, but the sales price increases to $2,500. As the difference in listening quality is slight at best, the extra price paid for the more expensive pair is clearly an example of *diminishing returns*.

In short, your conduct as a consumer relates to what you find important in life. With limited resources, but aspirations for the future, base your choices on thrift and discipline. As the years pass and net worth increases, modify your conduct accordingly, but keep in mind that these must be deliberate choices. Don't let advertising pressures or market manipulators preempt these decisions.

2

HOW TO AVOID MISFORTUNE

Don't trust to luck. Things
will only work out right if you
really know what you're doing.

Over the past several decades I've watched as the personal lives of a number of friends and acquaintances self-destructed. At first, each misfortune seemed unique, but in looking back I find common threads in these calamities. There are three factors which invariably lead to misery. Let me tell you how to avoid them.

1. **Beware the natural law of income and expenditures**. Innumerable works exist on the subject of income and expense as they relate to one another. Whether a scholarly dissertation on taxation, helpful hints on personal budget balancing, or a diatribe on welfare spending, certain elements of fact and fiction are often woven together to blur the obvious. The inability of many to separate financial illusion from reality is a national defect, and for an individual this failing can be a personal disaster. Of the many books on the subject, an exceptionally clear and enlightening one titled *The Law and the Profits* was published in 1960 by perhaps the most lucid writer of this century, the late English historian C. Northcote Parkinson. In it he postulated the maxim *expenditures invariably rise to meet and exceed available income*, and substantiated this as it relates both to organizations and individuals. It's this impulse to spend whatever is available that's the undoing of many otherwise rational persons.

The message is clear: To protect yourself, reject this tendency to spend up to and beyond your financial limit. A fine example was a close acquaintance, a wealthy "self-made" investor, who liked to boast of his thriftiness by saying that in his years as a young depression-era attorney he lived on only 30% of his income. (Interestingly, at the same time, his indolent son-in-law boasted, though more discreetly, that he, likewise, lived on 30% of the wealthy man's income. Perhaps there's a lesson to be learned here, but let's save it for another time.)

2.   **Do not commit to things you do not understand**. Of one thing you may be certain: You will often be called upon to make decisions for which you're unprepared. Whenever possible, defer your judgment to a more favorable time. There are instances, however, when you cannot wait. Under these circumstances you must make your decisions from the best information you can gather at the moment.

Frequently you must weigh the advice and recommendations of others, and the source of the counsel offered must be considered closely. It can be hazardous to place your confidence in persons merely because they're friends, relatives or professional advisors. The same can be said about the opinions of the wealthy, though it's not unusual to confuse financial success with knowledge. The line from the Broadway musical *Fiddler on the Roof* sums it up pretty nicely: " . . . because when you're rich, they think you really know."

Similarly, holders of credentials are no guaranteed source of sound advice. If they were, every licensed stockbroker would boast only prospering clients. This extends, as well, to persons with nationwide or even worldwide reputations of one sort or another. You may accept their guidance at your peril. Of course the advertising business might not function as effectively without the celebrity pitchman. For unknown reasons, the claimed benefits to the purchaser of a complex health insurance policy are presumed more credible when endorsed by an aging television talk show host or an illiterate sports celebrity. This is neither unique to the United States nor a recent phenomenon. The ability, for example, of royalty, the British equivalent of celebrity, to market products, was captured nicely in a Gilbert and Sullivan comic opera written over a century ago with the following lines spoken by the mythical Duchess of Plaza-Toro:

> "I write letters blatant
> On medicines patent—
> And use any other you mustn't;
> And vow my complexion
> Derives its perfection
> From somebody's soap—which it doesn't."
> [aside: "It *certainly* doesn't."]

In short, when required to make decisions on factors you consider less than reliable, disregard any advice, regardless of the source, not clearly understandable or with which you disagree, and try to postpone binding commitments until you acquire the missing information.

3.   The secret of success in virtually every endeavor is mastery of the details. If there is a single factor to explain why so many people fail in their undertakings, it's their inability, or perhaps unwillingness, to spend the time and energy to collect, evaluate and utilize information. Perhaps this is excusable, as there's little in the training of most of us that encourages close scrutiny of anything. It's my belief admonitions such as "You can't see the forest for the trees," and "We must step back to get the big picture," are mere rationalizations to avoid thought. The world is best viewed, not as a monolith to be comprehended through revelation, but rather, as a jigsaw puzzle in which a multitude of differently shaped and colored pieces are sorted and rotated while being fit together, often in unattached clusters, as the picture slowly forms. In short, the minutiae, an annoyance seemingly obscuring the subject, is often the actual substance, then assembled to *form* the subject. It's only by diligent investigation you can know what you're doing, learn what's happening to you, and control the situations confronting you. As once expressed: "When you know the details, no one can lie to you."

These are the simple—perhaps not so simple—ways to stay out of self-made trouble. Whenever you encounter a predicament, however benign it may at seem at first, try to reflect on these three rules. They can save you a heap of misery.

3

CHASING EXOTIC INVESTMENTS

The day after a big drop in the market,
a thousand stock analysts will explain
in detail what happened. But the day
before, not one of them had a clue.

Not long ago in the locker room of my club, an acquaintance I've spoken with over the years asked me a question: "Tell me, Al, what's your opinion on the future of the Euro as against the dollar?" Coming out of the blue, it took me by surprise. Though I'm familiar with the Euro, by which thirteen European Union nations currently maintain established conversion rates with their own national currencies, I didn't think he wanted a monetary analysis of the European Common Market. His focus seemed clear: making money through exchange rate speculation. I couldn't resist blurting out an answer: "If you want to know how to make a profit in buying or selling the Euro, you've asked the wrong guy!" That pretty well ended the conversation.

Since then I've given more thought to the subject. The fact is, I've never speculated in foreign currencies, nor even seriously considered it. It's an investment arena which takes special expertise. The trick to making money in this specialty is to know when to get in or get out. It's for this reason most currency speculators work for or with multinational banks, such as Deutsche Bank, Union Bank of Switzerland, and Citibank. Those who dabble in something that sophisticated without extensive background and experience in international finance are likely to lose their shirts. Even persons familiar with the intricacies of the foreign exchange market recognize the high degree of speculation inherent in a field where basic economic variables such as unemployment, productivity growth, and inflation play an important role in success or failure.

But foreign currency speculation aside, there is a more fundamental consideration: What sorts of investments are suitable for the average citizen? This is not a trivial question; it strikes at the heart of our uncertainties. As I've mentioned elsewhere in this book, my basic approach to investment—as well as to life—is mounted on an eleven-by-fourteen-inch parchment in a black frame, under glass, on my office wall. It is one of the many versions of Murphy's Law and reads:

Murphy's Law
(or the optimist creed)

"Nothing is as easy as it looks.
Everything takes longer than you expect.
And if anything can go wrong—it will
At the worst possible moment."

Although overstated for humor and effect, Murphy's Law expresses an intrinsic truth. It reminds us complexity is accompanied by consequences not easily foretold. Experience shows that as variables increase, more things go wrong, and as Murphy points out, unpredictability leads to problems which can cause a total breakdown of the system. Take note, the strength of a chain is no greater than its weakest link, and increasing the number of links increases the likelihood of failure. By analogy, the profitability of an investment program is no greater than its most vulnerable element. Similarly, increasing the number of elements increases the probability of mishap.

A specific example will help make the point. Presume you are involved in making trust deed loans (similar to mortgage loans) on single family dwellings in Santa Clara County, California. You're intimately familiar with the 1,290-square-mile area and its more than 1¾ million population, over half of it residing in the city of San Jose. With a vibrant though fluctuating economy, firmly rooted to the technology of Silicon Valley, centered in Sunnyvale and extending northward into Palo Alto, the residents of the area garner salaries to make loan payments which sustain property values. So long as the loans you make are fundamentally secure, as to creditworthiness of the borrowers and loan-to-value ratios of the securing homes, few troubles will arise.

Let's now consider a variation. You're asked to make a loan on a property in the community of Hollister, a 45-minute drive south into San Benito County. Though you may not realize it, you're out of your environment. With a predominantly minority population of 34,413, whose median annual income of $35,124 is derived largely from agriculture, Hollister cannot match the economy of its neighboring communities to the north. There are more things to go wrong. Might a surge in gasoline prices reduce the traffic passing through, thereby affecting local businesses? What will a crop failure do to local property values? It's clear: Lending here requires you anticipate unforeseen problems. Until you fully understand the economic factors that support Hollister, you'll be wise to decline making the loan.

This gets us to our main concern: What is a sound basis for placing your money at risk? It's that you avoid *exotic* investments. These I describe as ones over which you have little knowledge or control. Most assuredly, exchange rate speculation is an example of this. Yet another is the purchase of precious metals, such as gold or silver, if based merely upon the flow of hyperbole from persons who make their living promoting these commodities. This is not to suggest profits cannot be made from judicious speculation in precious metals, but most persons do not possess the capability to compete in such a market. A third example of exotic investment is acquisition of mutual funds, be they managed or index, on the sole presumption they must be good because everyone seems to invest in them. This, unfortunately, is the procedure by which the majority of Americans conduct their investment life—*investment by default*, so it seems—according to a formula that places no burden on the investor other than contribution of money. Because of it, the number of persons who reach retirement age with insufficient assets to sustain themselves are incalculable.

A final word is in order. The only sensible way to invest your dollars is by first investigating the field you plan to pursue, next familiarizing yourself with the details, and lastly easing into it slowly and cautiously as you feel your way along. As you gain experience, you'll know whether you've chosen a viable investment.

4

MARITAL WELLNESS: A VIEW FROM THE LEDGER

*If you aspire to rub elbows with
the rich and famous, expect to
end up with patches on your elbows.*

A magazine article I once read provided advice to the married and those about to be wed. I recognized the author as a well-known psychologist and specialist in the field. The article went on for five pages and touched on numerous topics including the importance of compatibility, factors in child raising, relations with in-laws, and general tips on keeping the marital magic alive. Although I found little to criticize on the subjects covered, one most important topic was ignored: the matter of money.

In general, marriage counseling is a profession reserved for those with special credentials that can include college degrees in family relations, certification by psychological or psychiatric boards, and accreditation through religious orders. Although I possess none of these qualifications, I'm not oblivious to what it takes to make a marriage tick, having witnessed many a successful one—

and too many unsuccessful ones, as well. To name a single element by which to separate the good from the bad, it's the eternal triumvirate: the husband, the wife, and the family finances. And in this category I possess the credentials, namely fifty years of a most pleasing married relationship together with a life-long specialty in money. It's for this reason I feel qualified to offer guidance on sustaining a successful union. Please stick with me as I spell it out.

As with so many subjects, we'd better begin before the beginning—which means *before* the nuptials. The brutal fact is there are a lot of persons out there who are simply unacceptable risks as marriage partners. In addition to the obvious ones—compulsive gamblers, chronic alcohol or drug users, psychotics, and other assorted weirdos—you must add those who exhibit unreliability. It's my belief a person's lifetime characteristics are largely developed by early adulthood. A man who cannot resist spending beyond his means upon graduation from college will be equally foolhardy a half century later. A woman whose checkbook is hopelessly out of balance on her twenty-first birthday may expect it to be similarly chaotic on the day she receives her first social security payment. In such ways, people don't really change much as they grow older. And these character traits can impose an intolerable strain on a marriage.

With this said, let me make my first recommendation. Recognizing that desirability as a marriage partner goes hand in hand with reliability in honoring financial obligations, you should not consider marrying without first obtaining a satisfactory credit check on your intended. Despite your infatuation, the warm glow will wear off quickly as reality sets in. Once you acquire a financially unreliable spouse, your predicament can be best described by the following tale. It involved a series of very early morning telephone calls by the same caller to a hotel lobby switchboard. The voice, sounding progressively more intoxicated with each call, asked repeatedly what time the bar opens, being advised each time the bar opens at 9:00 AM. In response to the same question at the 5:00 AM call, the desk employee answered sarcastically: "As I've told you before, the bar opens at nine, but what makes you think we'll let you in?" The voice responded in an almost unintelligible slur: "I don't want to get *in*. I want to get *out*."

In the marriage lottery, selecting the right partner is two-thirds the battle. Thereafter, it's mostly a matter of maintaining a steady course and avoiding the shoals. This requires you manage your family finances effectively. Reducing this to a single principle, it's far less important your earnings be large than that you habitually spend less than you earn. This can be a challenge, of course, as the market forces aren't designed to assist. So let me pass on three tips to help you prosper.

■ The misuse of credit cards is a national preoccupation, thanks in part to your friendly banker, with payment of interest by the American citizen a national outrage. If you want to understand what it's all about, consider how one typical institution, Bank of America, operates. For sums of money you place into their passbook savings account, you receive interest of ¼ percent annually. For sums of money they advance to you in cash on your credit card, you pay interest of 19.99 percent annually. Does this give you a hint as to how the playing field is tilted? We're now at the bare bones of the matter. My belief is a credit card has a single purpose—a convenience when neither check nor cash is handy. Most importantly, when the monthly statement arrives, pay the full cash balance before the date interest is charged. Follow this rule and the interest rate means nothing. If for any reason you cannot regulate your credit card use in this manner, destroy your cards, swear off cold turkey, and fashion your life accordingly.

■ There is no single product more forcefully promoted or representing such a substantial portion of disposable income than one's vehicle, and the potential for financial dilemma is all too real. From a logical viewpoint, it's easy to dispense the following advice on the purchase of a motor vehicle.

> 1) Don't buy anything you cannot pay for in hard cash without borrowings of any sort.

> 2) If a new car is not within your budget, search for a serviceable used one.

> 3) If continuing to use your present vehicle costs less than buying a replacement, don't make the change.

Unfortunately such advice is just that—easily dispensable. Social and psychological considerations make pressing demands. The need to sport a fashionable vehicle can be an obsession for many young, and not so young, persons. I recall my first financed new convertible with pride; by the time I made my last payment, it needed a new transmission and the top leaked. So, at this point you're entitled to a dispensation. Although my three rules may be logical and defensible, many of you simply will not conduct your lives in this Spartan fashion. Here's a next-best alternative: If you badly want a new car you cannot afford, consider a late model used car. These past years they all look alike anyway. And whatever you select, minimize your financing, and shop for the lowest interest rate. Except in the case of a new car subsidized by the manufacturer, it will generally not be the loan arranged by the auto dealer nor an unsecured bank loan. Borrowings secured by assets such as securities or an insurance policy are often available at lower rates. You may do even better from a credit union. Better yet, get a loan from a family member at little or no interest.

■ The first exposure to real estate for most of us is the home in which we live. Perhaps not surprisingly, if a youngster is raised in a rental unit, this becomes a factor in setting a way of life as an adult. In short, buying versus renting can be attitudinal. Let me express my bias from the onset: the goal is home ownership, and the sooner the better. This is important, for the purchase of a first residence is frequently the initial step in wealth building. At the very least, the longtime ownership of a home is often a key element in later life independence. Many a retiree who bought an inexpensive tract house with a minuscule down payment thirty or more years ago, and systematically paid off the mortgage one installment at a time, is today able to get by with little else than social security. But for a residence free of debt, this might not be possible.

Although there are other things I might add, you at least have a feel for the basic elements. Let me conclude my diatribe with the following admonition: Remember, marriage is a partnership of the most intimate sort, and as with all partnerships, mutual reliance and predictability is the cement which binds it firmly.

5

THE CASH VALUE OF HONESTY

*A reputation for honesty is a priceless
asset. If you haven't the ability to actually
be honest, at least try to look honest.*

While staring directly into the mirror, pose this question: Is this the face of an honest person? If the answer is even marginally affirmative, then try the follow-up query: Will honesty really enhance my overall life performance? The point is the value of honesty must be analyzed objectively rather than by the metaphor of the cherry tree reputedly chopped down by a young George Washington.

The real question to be asked is whether honesty is always the best policy. Some half century ago that versatile comedian Bob Hope starred in a situational comedy entitled *Nothing but the Truth*. In the picture Mr. Hope played the part of a man who entered into a wager requiring, for a period of twenty-four hours, he would tell no lies. Imagine the effect on his business and social life. At one point while at a dinner party, the hostess, a vain dowager, sought Hope's reassurance she looked no older than thirty. Hope attempted to sidestep the problem by answering in French, but his antagonist insisted the phrase be translated into English. The party ended abruptly with

Hope's translation that the hostess " . . . couldn't pass for thirty with a bag over her head."

The simple fact is the use of deceptive words and phrases—*euphemisms*, if you prefer—as well as outright lies is a time-honored tradition. The beginning of wisdom as well as the start in solving problems is to call things by their right names. Thus if a mentally defective child is called "exceptional," or a prison is described as a "correctional institution," despite the fact no real effort at correction is made, expect these verbal distortions to work against finding solutions. There are even more subtle ways reality is obscured through the way data is presented. The common admonition on the unreliability of statistics comes immediately to mind: "In this world there are lies, damned lies, and statistics." Not as well recognized is that the same perverted effect can be accomplished with graphical representation. As an example, a graph designed to show how the number of reported hate crimes changed over time can be rigged by the simple expedient of expanding or shrinking the abscissa and ordinate (x- and y-axes), so almost any impression can be given. While one graph may suggest a slow, almost imperceptible variance, the other can leave the impression hate exploded quickly to unprecedented levels, even though both provide the same information and, if the numbers are valid, technically they are equally accurate. Whether either distorts the picture is another matter altogether. You should recognize this practice is used constantly in an effort to shape public opinion to favor or oppose candidates, programs, legislation and commercial enterprises. Quite simply, lies and deception of this sort are used on a regular basis by the most "reputable" organizations for whatever purpose may be required at the time. If any of this is a surprise, you haven't been observant.

With this as a lead-in on public and institutional honesty, what must we demand of ourselves? It's appropriate to re-ask the question whether honesty is in fact the best policy. This cannot be settled with the expected affirmative answer provided by your scout troop leader or parish deacon, nor should you accept the cynical negative response most certainly gotten from a carnival sideshow operator or district alderman. Not until you come to terms with your own personal aspirations, family expectations, and demands of society, can you fashion a realistic code by which to live. In the final analysis, honesty for most people is rarely an absolute. Instead, it's relative and often selective. How relative and selective yours will be is an important life decision.

Let's now approach this head on. It's my firm conviction a reputation for impeccable honesty is among the most valuable assets you can possess. There are no limits to the doors that open and the opportunities afforded a man or woman whose words and actions can be trusted. Whether you're of truly high moral character, or possess the personal values of an eighteenth century London pickpocket, is not the issue. From a purely pragmatic frame of reference, conduct your affairs in a way your reliability can never be criticized. Note my stress is not on honesty per se, but on *reputation* for honesty, so if you cannot bring yourself to adhere to these standards, at least try to be discreet in your dishonesty. For those of you who fit into this category, take your cue from the late comedian George Burns who declared: "Sincerity is my strong point; I fake it masterfully." It's vital you not lose sight of the fact a sterling reputation is an irreplaceable commodity to be guarded carefully. And just as it's advantageous to be believed, strive to deal with others who likewise are believable. In short, recognize there's cash value in honesty.

6

EDUCATION: THE BOTTOM LINE

*The conventional wisdom is that
learning is something done to the
student, not by the student.*

In an earlier day—much earlier—I recall attending Ramsey Elementary School in St. Paul, Minnesota. During my first eight years of schooling I learned to read, write, and perform simple mathematical calculations. I also got a pretty fair background in history and geography, as well as other tidbits of information which found their way into the course of study. On the playground I developed some proficiency at hitting a softball with a wooden bat, maneuvering a hockey puck while on ice skates, dribbling a basketball across a court, and chasing my fellow students around the playground in an effort to "tag" them. My observations: As with most of my classmates, I mastered the subject matter, more or less, and consider the years reasonably well spent.

The prior paragraph describes education in the 1930s, a time generally known as "The Great Depression," when money was in short supply. Students provided their own books, paper and pencils, and other supplies. With school buses well beyond the means of any school district, we all traveled to school on foot, by bicycle or via the public bus or trolley. The educational backgrounds of our teachers—all of them poorly paid, to be sure—mattered little, with most of them the product of normal schools or teachers' colleges. Master's and doctoral degrees were unheard of. As I reflect back, I don't remember my teachers or a single word any of them ever spoke. Nonetheless, I managed to acquire a bit of learning. Over those school years I never encountered a counselor, a school bus driver, a teaching aide, a school psychologist, a grief therapist, a hate speech monitor, a campus guard, a union representative (teachers' unions did not exist), nor any administrative employees. With the exception of a lone clerk in the office and the janitor, everyone on the staff performed a teaching function; even the Principle and the school nurse taught a class or two. As nearly as I can tell, Ramsey Elementary operated on the proverbial *shoestring*, with funds generated at the local level, which didn't seem to detract from the learning imparted to those students who chose to exert some effort.

It's now many decades later and things are quite different. School teachers are well-paid *educators*, replete with credentials and multiple university degrees attesting to their educational expertise. No longer are curriculums limited to "the three Rs"—reading, writing and arithmetic. Far more exotic subjects are offered; perhaps "mandated" is a better term. Students are instructed in proper political attitudes, such as perfecting a correct display of respect for persons of other races and ethnicity. Competitiveness is also a concern, in that a student who fails to receive an academic honor may feel slighted. What better way is there to correct this unfairness than award no academic honors to anyone? And of course, another glaring unfairness is inequality among students. Why should some consistently come up with correct answers to questions and problems while others invariably fail to do so? The educational hierarchy wrestled with this problem for years. Their conclusion: Obviously a fundamental societal bias exists which must be eliminated. As students from well-to-do, educated, two-parent families, perform better than those from impoverished, uneducated, single-parent families, the latter must be favored in some fashion so each group will perform equally. The possibility one student may do better than another due to . . . an unspeakable term . . . "intellect," is a factor we dare not consider. Also unthinkable is the belief that certain individuals serve no purpose in a classroom. The decree from on high is clear and unwavering: All students are equally able and none may fail to successfully complete the prescribed course of study.

Based on these considerations, by the mid-Twentieth Century the nation's educational apparatus began to grind. Over the past half-century our nation stuffed more and more warm bodies into public classrooms while tapping its citizens for unbelievable sums of money to sustain this labyrinth. Until about a decade ago, most of the activity occurred at the state and local levels, as state legislatures, school boards and teachers' unions vied for control. During the past dozen years, however, the impetus moved to the federal government. Today Uncle Sam calls the shots, largely because it controls the purse strings. Under the direction of the federal government, through programs established by the *Elementary and Secondary Education Act of 2001*, known as *No Child Left Behind,* and the *American Recovery and Reinvestment Act of 2009,* known as *Race to the Top*, the youth of America are being groomed for scholastic excellence. Not only will all students master the academic subjects previously taught, but they'll rise to new heights, for it's decreed all students will excel. Intellectual limitations and academic ineptitude must no longer be a consideration. The official policy is such inabilities can be overcome when sufficient funds are appropriated and allocated, and in performing these feats the federal government will ensure that dollars are devoted for this purpose.

With that assurance, money began to flow. George Bush's *No Child Left Behind Act* established, among other things, grants to school districts for both teacher training and reading instruction, particularly among those schools with student test scores among the lowest. Under the law's key provision, schools must raise all students to proficiency levels in English-language and math by 2014. The result: As increasingly strict provisions and penalties of the law took effect, protests over the law grew in scores of states, where officials complained it required them to spend dollars they didn't have. As one example, more than half of California's low-income schools labeled as "failing" could lead to radical reforms such as state takeovers and charter conversion, and affect hundreds of millions of dollars in federal funding. The single biggest criticism was that the federal government failed to fully fund the program. Possibly so, but the *New York Times* reported in 2006, five years after the law's inception, that expenditures exceeded $23 billion in each of 2003, 2004 and 2005. So, as they say: What else is new?

When it came to spending money, President Bush proved to be modest. President Obama's *Race to the Top* opens the tap to an unending flow of innovation. Under this federal program, education becomes a performance-based contest through the award of points for satisfying various educational priorities. Points are earned by such devices as optimal distribution of teachers, closing gaps between socially diverse population groups, and developing of funding sources. Particular emphasis is placed on the lowest-achieving schools, with both massive targeting of funds as well as actual federal intervention. As might be expected, monitoring of the program is accomplished through a system of tests conceived by the federal government and imposed on local schools. And as expected, the federal intrusion into all aspects of schooling requires a corresponding infusion of federal dollars. As it's designed by politicians, not by persons with any experience in schooling, the billions of dollars already projected for the program will not likely meet the stated goals. As the late Illinois Senator Everett Dirksen once said, "A billion here, a billion there, and pretty soon you're talking about real money." Were he around today, *billion* becomes *trillion*.

These programs just described might be justified if the imposition of rules and the spending of money resulted in universal academic achievement. Unfortunately, this is not how it works. What actually happens is the participants learn to *game* the system. Let me offer an example which occurred in a California school district several years ago. Classroom teachers whose students earned higher test scores than the prior year became eligible for sizeable bonuses, compliments of the federal government. It takes little imagination to predict the outcome; the test scores of virtually every student in the district's several schools improved dramatically. The actual story only emerged because some disgruntled school employee blew the whistle. As a group, the teachers intercepted the students' answer sheets and changed wrong answers to correct ones before turning them in for grading. There's a term for this sort of activity; it's known as *human nature*. Any policy or program ignoring this basic trait is doomed to fail.

How can it be an establishment employing a huge work force and consuming a staggering amount of the nation's resources can be permitted to function in such a manner? It's because the school system is neither designed nor does it operate primarily to deliver an education to its students. Instruction in America is, at best, a peripheral goal of the public schools. In reality, the institution exists for the benefit of many diverse and conflicting groups including elected public officials, administrative hierarchy of the schools, the teachers and their representatives, non-credentialed employees, textbook publishers and distributors, and a host of groups and individuals too numerous to mention.

Let me now express what I believe to be the fundamental flaw afflicting the public schools. It's that the educational hierarchy embraces nearly every contrivance it can devise to *fix* the perceived imperfections while ignoring the basic flaw. The approaches include reducing class sizes, bonus pay to mentor teachers, more hours devoted to core subjects, established percentages of racial and ethnic minorities in each classroom, more highly credentialed teachers, increased emphasis on testing procedures, and a variety of programs regularly passing in and out of favor.

However, the fundamental defect afflicting the schools is the one not addressed. It's that many of the nation's schools are filled with students with no reason to be there. A great number of students are simply indifferent to education; with maturity this often improves. Others are in environments hostile to learning. In some locales a student displaying an interest in schooling can be physically assaulted by other youths in the community; this is certainly a challenging problem. Still other factors plaguing the system include parental indifference, student alcohol or drug use, and a variety of antisocial and anti-learning influences.

But by far the most disabling quality is mental inadequacy, for this is the sort of handicap which neither passes with time nor can be improved with community action. It's my belief a substantial portion of American youth regularly impressed into the classroom does not— and will never—possess the mental capacity to read, write or compute at any acceptable level. The untold billions of dollars expended in furthering the concept of *No Child Left Behind*, and *Race to the Top* serve no other purpose than justification for employing an ever greater army of professional educators. Accordingly, what is never considered is that *intellect*, the inherent capacity for rational thought, constitutes a factor in the educational process. In short, intelligence of the student is not a part of the equation.

I'll share with you a realization I eventually came to, though regularly denied by those in the schooling business. It's that scholastic achievement is not a collective activity, but rather a singular endeavor. Until this concept is at least grudgingly acknowledged by the educational establishment, no meaningful improvements will ever occur.

7

INVESTMENT AMERICAN STYLE

In the world of stock investments,
index funds are aggressively promoted for an
important reason: Whatever goes wrong,
you can't blame the promoter.

Over the years I've advocated methodical investment to whoever will listen. In newsletters I've describe techniques for profiting in real estate, corporate securities, and mortgage lending. I've somehow believed that with just a little guidance and encouragement, the average American will enthusiastically embrace investment opportunity. After all, we're an entrepreneurial lot, aren't we?

Perhaps my optimism is not well-founded. The more I view my fellow citizens, the more I'm convinced investment intensity is confined to a select group. An eagerness to pursue the road to prosperity is not found in most people. Let me describe why.

The average workingman or woman cannot view each day as an invitation to capitalize on opportunity.

Awake by six-thirty or seven, en route to the job by eight, the next nine or so hours are spent toiling at an assigned task or buried in established procedure. The benefit of any thought or effort goes to enrich persons mostly unknown to our employee.

Returning home by five or six that evening, the next several hours are devoted to dinner, the family, and the usual details of life. If by eight o'clock there's a lull in activities, the normal inclination is to plop in front of the television to view the latest episodes of *The Bachelorette*, *American Ninja Warrior* and *How I Met Your Mother*. By eleven it's off to bed, with the whole process beginning again the next morning. The weekends are normally spent catching up with what is missed during the working days. This may include an afternoon get-together with family or friends, a congenial dinner and movie on Saturday evening, church on Sunday morning, viewing a sporting event later in the day, and simply resting from the day's taxing activities. For most Americans, the week's 168 hours leaves no spare time to devote to such trivialities as planning an investment program, analyzing varied options, or actually managing a portfolio of securities.

What, then, of our average American's financial planning for that day when working years are over and retirement becomes a necessity? As you might guess, it must be a program requiring neither thought nor effort. It is, of course, America's traditional mediocrity: the open-end investment company known as the *mutual fund*. Since formation of the first such company in the United States in 1924, acceptance by the public grew to become universal. Quite simply, a mutual fund controls a pool of money provided by its shareholders which it invests in a portfolio of securities selected by the fund's managers. In recent decades they've proliferated like mushrooms, with over fifteen thousand registered funds now in existence—vastly more than the number of companies found on the New York Stock Exchange. They exist in near-infinite varieties offering almost every conceivable mix of securities.

For the potential investor with both limited expertise and assets, this type of investment seems to meet two important criteria: knowledgeable selection of securities and advantageous portfolio diversification. Though in theory the mutual fund meets the intended needs, theory and reality do not always match. Irrespective of the basic soundness of the investment advisory profession itself, the overwhelming fixation of most practitioners is on these funds, often dominated by *index* funds. There is no particular magic involved. These vehicles merely rise and fall with the general fortunes of the market. There are legitimate arguments why this approach makes sense for the advisors, if not always for their clients. A primary reason is that shares in a mutual fund now occupy an anointed status within both the investment and the legal communities. Within most limits, an advisor is held blameless if recommendations on this investment prove less than astute. And, as expected, with these funds being widely touted, natural client resistance is reduced. The result: an industry devoted to *investment by default*.

Although I maintain objections to the basic concept of mutual fund investment, I can't overcome a national obsession. The best I can do is express concern. Recognize this is an industry in which the placing of investors' money is, at best, a secondary consideration. The primary justification for their existence is to enable the operators to regularly skim a percentage of the gross assets of the funds while performing little more than marketing activities. The fact a substantial and growing percentage of the nation's assets is now committed to funds fuels a part of my concern. The rapid growth in the numbers and varieties of funds offered triggers more uneasiness. But it's the synergistic effect, coupled with basic human nature, which will guarantee unpredictable problems for investors.

Let me summarize with a grim prediction. What the future holds for the mutual fund industry is hard to say, but one thing is certain: The fortunes to be made, legally or otherwise, fuel an insidious attraction. At this point it appears to be a self-propelled labyrinth with few realistic controls, in the hands of persons who systematically milk the assets as a matter of course. As such, the American investor will surely experience misfortune of momentous proportion.

Now, with my dismal commentary on that portion of the corporate securities industry endorsed by the investment establishment, where do you go from here? I have a few thoughts, though they run counter to the advice you'll receive from most investment advisors. If we accept the premise that corporate stocks belong as a part of any overall investment program (and there are those who question this premise), initial guidelines must be set. I firmly believe the way to participate is simply through "specific stock choice." This is the method I chose some years ago when I took charge of a trust portfolio, which I then operated successfully for 21¾ years.

With some prior experience—not all of it good—together with a dose of selective reading and, most importantly, excellent continuing advice from a knowledgeable investor, the best approach seemed full investment in common stocks of well-established firms on the New York Stock Exchange. I selected companies in healthy industries with a history of stable or increasing earnings, a generous portion regularly passed on as dividends. I preferred only companies with reasonably low price-earnings (P-E) ratios, and reviewed the portfolio every several months so to dispose of those no longer meeting the criteria. The system worked reasonably well, in that both dividend income and asset value increased handsomely over time. Though certain aspects of the market changed in recent years, largely due to technology innovations, I believe *specific stock choice* is still the best approach.

Should you choose to emulate my stock investment method, there are a number of cautions I'll now pass on.

⇨ Do not, under any circumstances, authorize a brokerage establishment or individual stockbroker to maintain a discretionary account. The only person with authority to approve a transaction for your account is you.

⇨ Give thought to doing your business with a discount brokerage firm such as Charles Schwab or conducting your investments over the Internet. This is a method now quite popular. Compare the various commission schedules, and decide whether the savings is a fair trade-off for services lost.

⇨ Discourage your broker from offering buy or sell recommendations. You will be better served if such advice is in response to your specific queries.

⇨ Avoid involvement with anyone soliciting your business through telephone or mail. Rarely does any good come from such sources, with no limit to the potential for misfortune.

⇨   Keep abreast of the investment world.   An excellent source of information is subscription to the *Wall Street Journal*, published five days a week; *Barron's Weekly* is a fine supplemental source.   There is a wealth of valuable guidance in these two publications.

⇨   The Internet offers sites for rapidly researching the securities market.   One especially good source is Microsoft's www.msm.com.   Major brokerage firms also provide helpful sites.

⇨   For detailed information on a specific stock, check *Value Line Investment Survey*. The Company produces investment related periodical publications through its wholly owned subsidiary, Value Line Publishing LLC ("VLP"). VLP publishes in both print and electronic formats

⇨   At your earliest opportunity, read Andrew Tobias' *The Only Investment Guide You'll Ever Need*. The book, first published in 1978, is small, easily digestible and has been regularly revised since then. It is worth reading regardless of your prior experience in the market.

⇨   Do not trade in put and call options. They contain an element of risk you don't need. Only the seasoned speculator belongs anywhere in the vicinity.

⇨   What is true for options is doubly so for the commodities market. Perhaps Mr. Thorne, of *Kiss Me Kate* fame, cornered corn, but most such gamblers end up in the crib.

⇨   Unless you are a principal in a firm offering newly created stock to the public through an initial public offering (IPO), avoid acquisition of stock in this way—despite the source of the recommendation. Do not expect as an outsider there is a bonanza reserved for you. The profits will be distributed among the favored few—and you'll not be among them. In the spirit of the foundering private company, the IPO subscribes to the time-honored tradition: *Don't go broke . . . go public!*

⇨ Although both the options and the precious metals markets can be unprofitable for the unwary, an even surer way to lose money is in foreign-currency trading. You enter this venture at your peril. A humorous jingle aptly described the milieu a few years ago, which included the following lines.

> A more hazardous market
> is not to be found,
> for that's where the thieves
> and the swindlers abound.

⇨ Avoid any urge to involve yourself in the once popular sport known as *day trading*, which involves the purchase and subsequent sale of blocks of securities over the web, normally within hours of one another. It's widely touted as the common man's road to riches, with firms providing seminars on such trading, and on-line brokerage websites offering service at prices under $10 per trade. In its essence, it is a form of time-dependent arbitrage, but without the required assurance of *known* buy and sell values. As such, it becomes nothing more than pure speculation as to where a particular piece of the market will be at some time in the near future.

⇨ Finally, keep in mind the ground rules. Do not forget that human nature insures insider abuse, and in the field of securities it occurs without end.

You now have the concepts. There is little more I can add. With the examples conveyed, the cautions stressed, and the morals drawn, it's your job to see what part fits into your own personal investment plan.

8

HOLDING YOUR OWN AGAINST THE ESTABLISHMENT

You will either deal aggressively
with your problems or, most
assuredly, your problems will deal
aggressively with you.

Once, in an earlier time, this nation's entrepreneurial community showed consideration for its patrons. Marshall Field and John Wanamaker, founders of major nineteenth century department stores in Chicago and Philadelphia, both operated on the slogan "The customer is always right," a philosophy shared by many other businesses. An attitude favored customer satisfaction as an appropriate basis on which to conduct business. But those times are gone; commercial enterprise currently marches to a different drumbeat. The ethical standards once professed have been replaced by the canon of *enhanced shareholder value*. Whatever produces company profit is the sole criterion. Unfortunately there's nothing I can present here to change the way businesses operate, but perhaps I can provide guidance so you are not its victim. The following story, unhappily typical, provides enough specifics to demonstrate how redress is achieved.

An associate and I made an offer to purchase an apartment complex in Southern California. Its terms included a provision we assume the obligation of the existing mortgage loan on the property, subject to the noteholder's approval. In due course we submitted our assumption application, together with payment of $6,000, described as "$3,000 non-refundable processing fee and $3,000 deposit against legal costs." Our success with the lender is easily described in this summary of events. Jan 25: Submitted application with check; Jan 28: Check deposited by lender; Feb 1: Check cleared our bank; Feb 3: Notified by lender of application denial. Over the next several months we sought reconsideration, communicating repeatedly, all to no avail. By late June, we concluded our efforts. The loan was clearly unassumable, primarily because of a substantial prepayment penalty the lender hoped to collect through early payoff. We requested refund of our $6,000. This is when the skirmish began. Before going further, you must understand this lender was not a small regional firm with limited assets, nor a high-pressure bait-and-switch operator of questionable repute, but rather the mortgage loan arm of one of the nation's major lending institutions. Operating through offices in Atlanta, Georgia, it controls billions of dollars in mortgage loans throughout the country. Their reaction to our refund request is *standard operating procedure* by the nation's corporate community, illustrating how public dealings are conducted.

My first request, by certified mailing July 21, spelled out our justification for return of the full $6,000. An e-mail response arrived August 2, denying our entitlement to a refund. My second certified letter on August 8 restated my demand for full refund. With no reply, my third letter went out August 29 advising that "In the event this matter is not properly resolved by September 16, we will proceed with whatever action we deem appropriate." September 16 came and went with no response. I'll pause to set one matter straight. I never entertained the slightest expectation of a favorable reply, nor of my communication garnering a single dollar; that is not how corporate America operates. The return of money, however justified, does not result in *enhanced shareholder value*. The only way companies of this sort pay anything is when it is beaten out of them. It's customary for them to hide behind a wall of impenetrability, challenging you to locate a crack by which to get through. My three letters served nothing more than establish a basis for the next phase, that being a lawsuit. Here is where strategy is involved. The logical way to proceed is with a speedy and low-cost small claims action. Unfortunately, that particular court's maximum claim limit was $5,000, and I intended not writing off any part of our entitlement. However, a municipal court suit for the full $6,000 would entail objectionable costs, formality, and uncertainty. The logical answer: instituting separate small claims actions by my associate and me, each for $3,000. We filed those lawsuits September 19, both cases to be heard November 22 in a courtroom in Santa Ana, California. With the stage set, the next action would be theirs.

Let's pause once again and put ourselves into the mortgage lender's head. How will the defense be conducted? California law provides in small claims actions the defendant must personally appear to respond to the charges, in this case meaning an authorized corporate official. Neither an attorney nor third-party representative may substitute. What's the practical effect? A knowledgeable corporate representative must travel from Georgia, prepared to competently present a defense. This requires expenditure of airline fares, hotel accommodations, the loss of at least two days' executive productivity, and the accompanying inconvenience, all to haggle over $6,000. Perhaps this explains why I received a telephone call from the firm's legal representative on October 11 proposing to settle the matter for $3,000. I politely suggested $6,000 as more appropriate. On November 15 I received the next call, with a $4,500 offer that I cordially declined. Their November 16 call elicited the magic number, and within hours I received a faxed settlement agreement. Their $6,000 cashier's check arrived the day after Thanksgiving.

This story deserves some concluding thoughts. Why might a presumably honest corporate employee, who would never consider cheating a local vendor, be a party to flagrant abuse of the general public? I believe it to be a matter of *proximity*. What we will not do in face-to-face encounters with persons we know is permissible with strangers at a distance. So, consider the effects of outsourcing. How will a corporate representative in Calcutta deal with a customer in Seattle? And finally, what is the moral of this tale? It's simply that if you are to prevail against corporate indifference, you must display perseverance. The establishment correctly expects most persons to lose interest and give up. It's your job to disappoint them.

9

SURVIVAL IN TOUGH TIMES: SMART SHOPPING

If a vendor must buy a dozen
pages of advertising to say how
wonderful its product is, it can't be.

When economic times are good, you may be inclined to shop with little regard for price or value. But when conditions turn sour, as they have for many Americans, it's another story. The advertising industry is devoted to identifying what citizens consider significant. Even more so, the market manipulators create those choices. With customers in shorter supply and lesser sums to be spent, the competition is as fierce as it is grotesque. As your dollars must be stretched longer and harder, you'd better spend each of them wisely.

What brand of watch do you wear? Whether a top-of-the-line Rolex Oysterquartz Datejust, a fashionable Cartier, a respectable Bulova, or an economy Timex, recognize all are fine devices and none fail to keep excellent time. Except for the archaic Rolex, all are battery-operated, with a similar quartz movement; the day of the mechanical Swiss movement is a thing of the past. The current models all do a better job than the "precision" pocket watch your Great-grand-uncle Elmo used as an engineer on the Lackawanna Railroad. The only justification for a high-priced model is self-image and the *illusion* of prosperity. The value of these qualities is overrated.

And while on the subject of small mechanical devices which serve a need, consider the hyperbole employed by one firm to convince us of the importance of a $600 ballpoint pen. The arguments include an appreciation of beauty and workmanship, the profound emotional experience you receive utilizing a fine writing implement, and the implication you will be admired by clients and associates for your taste and culture. A number of competing firms aggressively promote substantially identical versions, with radio and television ads regularly employed. There are two fascinating aspects of this campaign, the first that the hired pitchmen manage to keep a straight face while reading their lines. The other is that anyone not certifiably demented actually believes a word of it. Nonetheless, for whatever reason, the pens enjoy a market. On a personal note, the pen in my shirt pocket, with probable value of about 29¢, carries the somewhat worn inscription "Resdeck Plumbing, Redondo Beach, Calif, *Your problems are our problems*." In the past month I used it to sign a variety of documents which, to borrow a line from one of those ads, were truly "admired by my associates."

What can be said about wristwatches and ballpoint pens is equally true as to other highly promoted products. These include magazine offerings, timeshare projects, $300 per ounce bottles of perfume, Las Vegas weekend getaways, and the purchase of lottery tickets, to name just a few.   As a rule of thumb, the more overpriced the merchandise, the more innovative its promotion. Perhaps there is a connection, if only because moderately priced items representing honest value incur less sales resistance, so need not be touted with such vigor.   Reflect, for a moment, on the recognizable voices and faces making the outrageous claims. If there's a benefit to this, perhaps it's the association of certain marketing celebrities with a product of any sort. You're saved the effort of analyzing the offering; you may reject it out of hand.

Let me offer a few other examples of money badly spent. This behavior pattern multiplied and added up over a lifetime represents a fair chunk of your earnings.

Twenty-four rolls of a popular brand of toilet paper is available at Walmart for $10.19. Six rolls of the same product, selling at a major market for $6.46, is easily dropped into a shopping cart.   The two-hundred-fifty percent markup doesn't seem to bother many housewives, though it should.

An envelope containing three sheets of paper arrived in the mail yesterday with two 46¢ stamps—total: 92¢. At two ounces, its correct charge is 66¢. Actually it weighed just under an ounce, so the sender evidently guessed on the high side. Much correspondence arrives with excess postage—a lazy and expensive way to send mail. As you might guess, my desk drawer contains a small sixteen-ounce postal scale. I've owned this little device since 1962 when postage was 4¢ per ounce. Over the years the scale paid for itself a thousand times.

And speaking of envelopes and paper supplies, where might they be bought cheaply? Except for top-grade rag content or custom-engraved stock, avoid the stationery stores. Even the major discounters are not the places to go. A little comparison shopping reveals paper supply houses offer the lowest prices, and most are open to the general public.

When you fill your car with gasoline, does the lesser-priced regular grade or the higher-priced premium grade end up in your tank? Don't base your decision on assurances by the service station manager promoting the more expensive fuel, but on performance you can actually experience. The fundamental difference between the two grades is octane number—burning speed—when in earlier years slower burning helped prevent engine "knock." Because of the lower compression ratios of today's cars, most function satisfactorily on 87-octane fuel. The test is simple to conduct. With the lower octane gas in your tank, accelerate up a slight grade in drive gear. If you experience no unrelenting "pinging" of the engine, then the lower octane gas is working well and you may save yourself the cost of the more expensive fuel.

I hope this message is coming across clearly. You're not well advised when you make your buying decisions based on urging from shopkeepers or exhortation from advertising. Sharpen your buying habits with a healthy dose of skepticism. Look closely at the product, read the specifications, verify the quality, and compare prices. You'll often find what is claimed is not what is offered. In most of your purchases you are less familiar with a product than are its vendors. You can overcome this disadvantage with a little effort and by educating yourself. The results are cumulative and your performance will improve with time.

10

THE SEVEN FUNDAMENTALS OF SOUND INVESTMENT

I've never taken a single course in either business or economics, nor am I acquainted with any Certified Financial Planners. I credit this as a factor in never having lost my shirt.

Over nearly five decades of involvement in investments, both participating in and observing, I've witnessed about every variation imaginable. During this period I've also surveyed endless advice and recommendations on the subject. Yet, despite the overwhelming amount of information available, the actual principles of investment are few in number and basic in their application. Generally, if you can cut through the maze surrounding a proposal or offering, the elements upon which its probable success or failure relies becomes easily observed. To this end, I'd like to discuss the seven fundamental factors which govern investment.

1. Consider your Comfort Level. Whatever your selected endeavor, take into consideration your personal abilities and limitations. If, for example, you function well with people in a down-to-earth business setting and enjoy the challenge of making repairs and improvements to real property, you might be a natural in owning and managing apartment units. However, if you consider the prospect of tenant interaction repugnant, and regard property maintenance as a drag, you'll do yourself no favor by entering the field. Similarly, if you find a corporation's annual report intriguing, and eagerly scrutinize analysts' reviews in the evaluation of public companies (there really are such people), you could find success in building and maintaining an active and profitable securities portfolio. But for those of you who regard corporate securities a bore, or for whom ownership of a share of stock that declines in value causes mental anguish, you're probably better off staying clear of the market.

2. Beware of Needless Complexity. Never forget, as matters become increasingly complex, there are more things to go wrong. Therefore, if you choose to purchase subordinated debentures issued by a firm which manufactures and markets highly specialized golf clubs, the safety of your investment will be subject to successful management of the company, competition by other firms, the popularity of golf, and many other variables I can't even imagine. By contrast, when loaning money to a homeowner with good credit and substantial home equity, secured by a mortgage, there is far less uncertainty. As the prevailing theory goes, reward increases with risk, so you'd expect interest paid on the debenture to be far greater than on the mortgage loan. But in real life it doesn't always work that way. For this reason, in every case it's your job to consider the complexities, analyze the risk, and decide whether the return is adequate.

3. Be Certain the Numbers Make Sense. When presented with an investment proposal, together with figures purporting to show how advantageous it will be, the first thing to consider is whether the numbers are reasonable. Do they seem to make sense? I'll give you an actual example. I recently analyzed the purchase of an annual 1-week interval at a *timeshare* project for a friend, the specific property being a 750 sq ft, 2-bedroom condominium in a resort complex in the Coachella Valley area of Southern California. The terms: $14,500 price, 20% down payment, monthly mortgage installments $97.90 for 15 years, and $47.50 monthly toward taxes, insurance, maintenance, and supervision. Although my friend could easily afford the $2,900 down and $1,745 a year carrying cost, I pointed out an identical unit at the resort rented at a daily rate of $125. Why purchase if the cost of a week's stay is only $903, with no initial investment or mortgage burden? To conclude my argument I quickly calculated, with buyers for each of the year's 52 weeks obtained under the same terms, the *timeshare* association receives $754,000 in sales revenue plus $29,640 in annual payments for a single unit. Adding insult to injury, similarly sized condominiums a few miles away garnered a market price of only $195,000. As you might guess, my friend expressed no further interest in the project.

4. Identify the Source of Profitability. If anything constitutes the heart of an investment, it's the reasonable assurance it will generate a benefit of some sort over a period of time. In the case of corporate stock, this is the systematic payment of a dividend and/or appreciation in share value. For the ownership of commercial real estate, it means an expectation the property will generate a net cash flow as well as experience some value enhancement. Note the basis for value is not the benefit generated, but rather the "reasonable assurance" of this benefit. This may seem illogical, but it's significant. In each case, value is determined by careful analysis of the underlying operations. To make the point, even though it may pay its holder a fortune, a lottery ticket possesses no definable value. There can be no reasonable assurance it will deliver anything. And yet this gambling mentality often takes charge in establishing whole industries. As a striking example, consider America's technology firms in the years leading up to their 2000 collapse. Many of those companies experienced phenomenal increases in common stock price despite the fact they neither generated income, produced viable products, nor offered future promise. No reasonably anticipated benefits existed; any value relied on pure speculation. By contrast, as I began purchasing previously foreclosed-upon condominiums in 1995 from banks and government agencies in then-bankrupt Orange County, California. The rental market assured an annual 16% return on the less-than-replacement-cost purchase prices. Whether or not the properties might one day appreciate in value seemed almost unimportant. The predictable cash return justified any long term risk. It worked nicely and the six-fold increase in market value over the following ten years, almost an afterthought, proved to be massive frosting on the cake.

5. Verify the Information. Though you obviously realize it's unwise to make an investment without verifying all the pertinent details, this is more easily said than done. One case in point is the selecting of corporate securities. You're familiar with the information firms such as Value Line and Standard & Poor's provide when advising on the soundness of a company. However, you can't ignore the fact that shortly before Enron Corporation filed in Chapter 11 Bankruptcy on December 2, 2001, all the rating services gave the company's stock a high grade. Similarly, the mutual-fund monitoring service, Morningstar, evaluates funds on the basis of risk and performance. Nonetheless, when in the autumn of 2003, many of the funds experienced a melt-down amidst revelations of fraud, Morningstar provided no advance warnings. If these professional evaluators found themselves so easily fooled, what are your chances? Of course, there's no pat answer to this question. Each of us must recognize our own limitations. One response is to hedge our bet with diversity. Thus, instead of heavy investment in each of only a few stocks, we'll spread our choices to minimize the risk if one or two of them go sour. One prominent radio advisor urges no more than four percent of a person's portfolio be placed in any one security. A second technique, and one I favor, is to avoid the sort of investments which require reliance on either company reports or rating services. It means, when examining an operation, sufficient details can be understood and relied upon from independent sources. Above all, each element of the information must be clear enough so it can be corroborated by common sense. This is the approach of one very successful investor, Warren Buffet, Chairman of Berkshire Hathaway, who escaped the collapse of technology stocks in 2000. He explained he abstained from investing in that sector because he didn't understand it.

6. Arrange for Adequate Security. In any investment it's always advisable if you can cover downside risk with some sort of security. There's no better example of this principle than in the lending business. The difference between unsecured debt, such as a signature loan, and an obligation secured by a mortgage—a document permitting the lender to seize a parcel of property by foreclosure—can mean the difference between wipeout and full recompense. To hew the line even more cautiously, we might further distinguish between mortgage loans secured by owner-occupied single family homes versus those secured by apartment houses. In the event of loan default in the former instance, the owners may avail themselves of various delaying tactics including prolonged bankruptcy action. If the home equity securing the loan is inadequate, the lender may suffer. But with an apartment loan in many judicial districts, the courts will often award receivership, permitting the lender to commandeer the building and collect the rents during the foreclosure period. It is this option which can make the difference between loss and gain. It goes without saying, of course, the more clearly you understand the details of an endeavor, the better you're able to prepare for what might go wrong.

7. Search Carefully for any Overriding Defect. The final thing you must do before making a financial commitment is to step back and view it for any element that seriously detracts from its viability. Is there some specific defect which might nullify an otherwise inviting opportunity? As an example, I'll offer a testimonial. In 1993, at the depth of a Southern California real estate recession—admittedly far less disastrous than the *Great Recession* (in reality, a depression) we witnessed in more recent years—I encountered an opportunity to purchase a 38-unit apartment building in Riverside County. The owner, a bank that acquired it in a prior foreclosure, wanted to unload. From my perspective, almost everything seemed ideal. With only six units occupied, and those by evictable deadbeats, I intended to secure tenancy of my choice. Despite its abysmal physical condition, other buildings in the locale looked pretty good. And best of all, the bank offered to make a 95% loan-to-facilitate at a purchase price of only three times the building's annual potential rent schedule—virtually a "steal." As I said, everything seemed ideal—almost. There was, however, one fly in the ointment: A partner came with the property. For reasons I never fully understood, the bank seemed bound to a commitment by which a former holder of interest retain an undivided fifty percent beneficial ownership interest with whoever should purchase the property. Thus, I'd be only half-owner, with all the inherent limitations. To make a long and traumatic story very short, I met the prospective *partner*, ordered a credit check, and ran a five-county judicial search on him. His record proved to be as bad as I perceived him. Although the property offered the potential of quadrupling in value over a few years, I reluctantly passed up the purchase. I've never regretted my decision, though I do shudder somewhat when I think back at the lost opportunity.

Let me sum things up. Successful investment can be challenging, but need not be overwhelming. Apply these seven fundamentals to each investment opportunity you encounter and you'll quickly eliminate those with fatal flaws. But keep in mind you'll not be popular with whoever is advocating your participation. It's unhappily true most investments are promoted by interested parties who exaggerate benefits and minimize risks. My advice: Ignore the pitch and rely on your own analysis and instincts. And remember always if it doesn't make sense to *you,* it doesn't make sense.

11

THE ECONOMICS
OF A HABIT

Cancer cures smoking.

A few days ago, while waiting in line at a Rite Aid drug store, I watched the fellow directly ahead of me, a young man about eighteen, purchase a package of Marlboro cigarettes. The price caught my attention: $6.47. Though I once smoked two packs a day, it was a long time ago. To give you an idea *how* long ago, my brand, Raleigh's, then sold for $1.39 a carton. After quitting, I sort of lost track of it, never imagining how expensive the habit might become. This revelation came as a real surprise.

For some reason, when I left the store I didn't dismiss the matter from my mind. I visualized this fellow making his daily purchase over the years, passing through young adulthood, middle age, and finally into the domain of senior citizenship, while continuing to emit a never-ending stream of smoke. Actually, the vision came easily, as several of my friends and acquaintances are still users after more than forty years. Perhaps my fellow oldsters deserved scrutiny before I focused on this hapless teenager, but it didn't register the same way. You see, my generation can be excused for its nicotine use. Note that at an earlier time cigarettes were cheap, plentiful and promoted as the last word in glamour. We all admired our president, Franklin D. Roosevelt, as he posed with his cigarette holder clenched firmly between his teeth and a smile on his lips. But times have changed. As the tobacco industry is deluged with lawsuits and restrictive legislation, while the smokers are shunted from space to space, smoking today is more the province of the outcast than the idol.

At this point I could launch into a dissertation on the evils of tobacco, but that's not my intent. Instead, I want to share some financial hallucinations: the revelation of what cigarette indulgence represents in hard dollars. The numbers are fascinating, so stick with me as I craft the scenario.

To begin with, the full cost of a pack is *not* $6.47. Both state, county and local sales taxes will be added—8 percent here in Orange County, California—so the customer actually hands over $7.00. However, this doesn't tell the whole story. The real question becomes: What earnings must one generate to cover the purchase price? Unfortunately few of us get to keep our whole salary. Big brother, Uncle Sam, and sometimes his sidekick, the state tax collector, first take their cut. We only pocket what's left over. How much, then, did our young friend earn so to fork over $7.00? We'll make a presumption here; let's say he pulls down the not unreasonable wage of $15 an hour. This puts him in the 15 percent federal income tax bracket, the 6 percent California bracket, and his 7.65% FICA hit. At his effective 28.65% tax bracket, he gets to keep 71.35% of his pay. A bit of math tells us it takes $9.81 of his earnings to buy that pack of smokes. As an aside, he's fortunate he doesn't live in New York; a pack there costs twice what it does in California.

If the story ended here, we might simply philosophize as to whether the pleasure of smoking—we'll presume a pack a day—offsets the financial cost, irrespective of any health considerations. Well, I'm sorry, the story doesn't end here. We're about to take a financial excursion to see what seven bucks a day really means. And since I'm the tour director, I get to steer.

The analysis starts on an 18th birthday, contemplates $7.00 per day, deposited monthly into a money market account of a self-directed Roth Individual Retirement Account (Roth IRA) with a stockbrokerage firm continuing until the 65th year. During this time, the money will be gainfully employed—and I'll tell you how. At the end of each year, any cash in the account is invested in corporate bonds. If done properly over the long haul, a 5% return, compounded semiannually, is not unreasonable.

Perhaps the prospect of an annual 5% return fails to impress you. If so, it's because you can't visualize the compounding effect. What occurs, simply, is when paid, the interest earns interest, which in turn earns interest, which in turn . . . I think you get the picture. The reality is in 47 years, $7.00 per day grows to $431,000, with no taxes to be owed as you begin to withdraw. That's not a bad way to begin retirement.

At this point I'll fess up and admit to having written this as much to discourage smoking as to counsel investment. If I can encourage anyone to kick the weed, I certainly will. Perhaps the following testimonial will convince a few of you to swear off.

◆　　◆　　◆

SIR WALTER REVISITED

As nearly as I recall, I looked pretty macho back in the '40s—it was probably the way my cigarette hung from the left side of my mouth, with the ¾-inch ash neatly balanced at the tip.

As a 2-pack-a-day smoker, the habit reinforcements are still vivid in my memory. At that time smoking enjoyed popular support, thanks to regular promotion by such celebrities as Humphrey Bogart and Ronald Reagan, and the Surgeon General had yet to issue a report declaring it a health hazard. Though the ads of the day proudly proclaimed such nonsense as "Not a cough in a carload," we unsophisticated teen-agers knew instinctively we were breathing something harmful. Raleigh, the brand several of us smoked, came with a coupon attached to each package which, when enough were collected, could be exchanged for various prizes. Our standard gallows humor was we were saving up for an iron lung.

Many persons wise up at some point in life, my awakening coming shortly after my nineteenth birthday on December 10, 1949. There's no doubt in my mind that had my cigarette use continued, I'd now be long dead. Perhaps this isn't important from an overview of human history, but it certainly has significance for me.

Most of us who became hooked on the weed started our use at an early age, thanks in part to the effective targeting by the tobacco industry of children in the eleven-to-fourteen age group. And make no mistake—it was effective. The combination of romantic images, reinforced with seductive Kool billboards, delusions of grandeur perpetuated with visions of an unfiltered John Wayne, and the constant reminder of personal inadequacy assuaged only by a sense of oneness with the Marlboro Man, was what enabled the tobacco companies to declare healthy quarterly stock dividends.

It's also true many of us who kicked the habit did so without extensive or expensive treatment programs. It's hard to say what's required for a smoker to set tobacco aside, as different people respond to different stimuli. The threat of imminent death by cancer is sufficient for some, while others continue to puff through a plastic tube inserted in their trachea after the malignant larynx has been surgically removed. It's a very personal matter, and as with all addictions—yes, *all* addictions—until the individual decides to quit, it will not happen. Only when the basic psyche finds itself at cross-purposes with a habit, will the practice end. It's for this reason that treatment efforts for all sorts of substance-abuse are normally ineffective. Whether it be alcohol recovery, encouraged and paid for by family members, or court-ordered drug rehabilitation, without the resolve by the addict it will come to nothing. It has long been my suspicion the practitioners who operate such facilities are keenly aware of this, and count on repeated failures as the basis for continuing profitability. The last thing Ms. Helga Hammerlock, owner/operator of *The Dry-Out Emporium,* really wants is that any of her collection of recyclable sots actually give up the bottle.

Another aspect of tobacco has to do with its physiological effect. Much research has been conducted and over two hundred chemical substances, some clearly carcinogenic, have been identified as smoke ingredients. For many years cigarette makers have stressed filtration and its effect in reducing tar and nicotine. The potency of every chemical agent, from trace amounts of benzene and formaldehyde to the products of the chemically treated paper, is vigorously debated. It has even been suggested, perhaps with justification, that a cigarette high in nicotine would be the safest, in that the addict can get the required fix with the least exposure to other harmful ingredients.

In the discussion, one thing rarely mentioned is the agent which may be the most deadly ingredient of all: the tobacco itself. It's recognized in research circles the tobacco leaf is surprisingly rich in radioactivity, with evidence the sources are ingredients of the phosphate fertilizer in which the tobacco is grown. The principal culprits seem to be two radioactive isotopes that decay through beta emission, and which hang around in a pretty active state for the better part of a half-century. These beta particles have a slight penetrating ability, so that when the tobacco smoke deposits its ingredients on the surface of a lung, the tissue nearby will be bombarded for years with ionizing radiation: a recognized cause of molecular mutation with its potential for malignancy. There's an excellent likelihood *this*, rather than chemical factors, is the primary cause of lung cancer. If so, no filter which permits the smoke containing the vaporized tobacco leaf to pass through, regardless of the reduction in pollutants, can be effective. Inasmuch as the smoke is the one thing which must get through if there's to be gratification for the smoker, safety becomes unobtainable. Only the ultimate filter which lets *nothing* through could be claimed to eliminate all health hazard, and trying to take a drag through that would probably result in a double hernia.

My sympathy goes out to today's youthful generation. With the popularity of smoke-free areas, the public's contempt for the smoker, and a tobacco industry fighting for survival, most will find it tough developing the nonchalant swagger I perfected a half-century ago. And as they puff, I'm reminded of the popular lament: *Ve ist too soon old und too late schmart.*

12

PANIC TIME: PROBLEMS THAT SPELL TROUBLE

Life is an enterprise in which much can go wrong—and in time, it will.

With luck, most of us match our family income to our costs of living and come out ahead of the game. At times, of course, we may experience a run of expenses, often unanticipated, causing us to dip into savings or even float a temporary loan to tide us over. As long as the problems are resolvable and the costs controllable, we can usually work our way out of the difficulty. There are, however, circumstances which spell real trouble. Let's look at three of these situations to see what can go wrong and how they may be tackled.

1) Family illness. One of the principal reasons for economic hardship, often resulting in the filing of personal bankruptcy, is serious family illness. Medical services are expensive. It's easily possible for an injury or ailment to result in major surgery and a hospital stay to generate bills exceeding one hundred thousand dollars. This is an expense that, without adequate medical insurance, can strain any budget. Comprehensive medical policies are costly, with premiums continuing to rise. Cost-saving benefits may be realized from Obamacare, but are as yet unknown, and the entire health care industry is undergoing cataclysmic change. In short, sickness can break the bank.

What then is the solution? Obviously you can't avoid medical risk by simple healthful living . . . though you'd nonetheless be wise to avoid bungee jumping and crocodile wrestling. I have a better suggestion. It's a device known as *catastrophic health insurance*. The concept is basic. It's an insurance policy with a high deductible and a low monthly premium. Under this program, you determine in advance what medical expense you are willing and able to personally fund. This sets the policy limits which vary depending on the plan you select. One example, an Aetna policy for a 25-year-old female with an $86 per month premium, offers a $5,000 annual deductible and 30 percent coinsurance thereafter, with an out-of-pocket limit of $7,500, and $1 million maximum benefit, or "cap." Alternatives are available where the premium rises as the deductible falls, and vice versa. Admittedly, this may not qualify as nirvana, but it can avoid catastrophic expenses that might wipe you out.

    2) Loss of employment. A second major cause of financial distress is job loss. It's reported more than 60 percent of Americans cannot meet regular living expenses within 30 days following termination of their salaries. If not for unemployment benefits, government food and shelter programs, and charitable organizations, the percentage might be even higher. And there is more to joblessness than financial hardship. A person's inability to sustain a livelihood is debilitating. The loss of personal self-worth can be traumatic. In any event, financial self-sufficiency is the goal, with or without a job.

As with so many other aspects of life, we'd do well to anticipate misfortune and try to prepare for it. Plan for a loss of employment is before the loss occurs. And the best way to insure you'll not be caught short is to possess sufficient savings set aside to handle your living expenses for a reasonable period of time. By living expenses, this must include all your normal expenditures for housing, utilities, transportation, food, insurance, and debt payments, though you need not include savings, investment programs, charitable contributions, or entertainment. There are differences of opinion as to the specified time period, some as short as three months, with most advisors recommending six months. My personal belief is six months is a bare minimum. You'll be better served with a nest egg sufficient to maintain yourself in the style to which you've become accustomed for a full twelve months. As to the form of the assets, three months of your anticipated living expenses should be in a bank money market account, drawing the best FDIC-insured interest available—I admit it's currently pathetic. Another three months of your stash may be in 3-month bank CDs. For the balance of the funds, a 6-month CDs is suitable. Under no circumstances may these assets be exposed to risk of any sort. This means nothing which may experience market fluctuation, including but not limited to stocks, corporate bonds, or mutual funds. It's hard, cold, moola you want, for when the going gets tough, cash is king.

3) Marital breakup. As unpleasant as it may be, the solemn oath so frequently uttered—*To love, honor, and obey* (or *cherish*, depending upon gender), *till death do us part*—is not always a gilt-edged guarantee. When, as so frequently happens, a parting of the ways occurs, it's often accompanied by accusations and recriminations, followed thereafter with a precipitous drop in income. Statistics reveal the wife is usually the bigger loser, though with unanticipated legal costs, creation of a second household, and change in lifestyle, both spouses normally experience the financial fallout.

Once again, advanced planning may save the day. The device used is a premarital agreement, often known as a "prenuptial agreement" or "prenup," which is simply a written contract created by two persons before they wed. Typically, these agreements list the assets each possesses at the time of marriage and specify the respective property rights they will enjoy during marriage and the intended disposition of assets in the event of a divorce or separation. Despite what you've heard, a prenup is not exclusively for the wealthy. When properly drawn, it can prove valuable to persons of modest means. However, proper drafting is the key to its use. Generally, state law governs enforceability, so the contract must be drafted by a competent attorney to insure interpretation as intended. Once in place, the newlyweds may proceed with their lives, secure in the knowledge any future marital difficulty will not carry with it the seeds of financial ruin.

One last comment is in order. With these three potential cataclysms—illness, job loss, and marital breakup—minimized, pure chance becomes less a factor in your prosperity. Now you need only concentrate on conducting your financial life sensibly. Good luck and smooth sailing.

13

TIPS FOR THE ASPIRING HOMEOWNER

I favor vigorous and unbridled real estate
development in all areas—except
within ten miles of my waterfront home.

Home ownership, a vital element in what constitutes *The American Dream*, is certainly a blessing. Unfortunately, it also contains the seeds of what can be financial misfortune, perhaps never more graphically depicted than in a 1986 Steven Spielberg movie, *The Money Pit*, starring Tom Hanks and Shelley Long, in which a young couple experiences every calamity possible in remodeling a dilapidated house. With the aim of helping aspiring homeowners avoid some common errors, I want to pass on seven tips.

1. Pick the right area. Perhaps the most overused phrase in real estate is: "The three most important factors in real estate are location, location, and location." This happens to be true, but rarely does advice follow its utterance. What this means in practical terms is you select your home in an area that exhibits pride of ownership, few if any slum properties, an absence of nearby vacant commercial spaces, neighborhood schools with high performance ratings, and a community with a low crime rate. Whatever cannot be noted by inspection is readily available from a variety of sources. And as to the house itself, though it's always nice to get a pretty one, the location is the main concern. I've always operated on the premise the worst house in the best neighborhood beats the best house in the worst neighborhood.

2.   Don't stretch beyond your means. It's common knowledge in the real estate industry tenants tend to rent less expensive residences than they can afford, whereas homebuyers customarily reach for the moon—and beyond. Perhaps it's a psychological acknowledgement of intentions: temporary vs. permanent. Regardless, there is an approach toward life I advocate, known as *sandbagging*. It suggests you don't commit to obligations which may strain your limits. It's far more sensible you obligate yourself to *less* than you think you can handle, this in recognition of the brutal nature of reality. For those of you who need it spelled out in simpler terms: Choose a cheaper home than you can afford.

3.   Avoid a hazardous mortgage. At no time in the past forty years have mortgage interest rates been as low as they are currently, nor does it seem likely they will drop lower. Though that doesn't necessarily mean rates will rise, the odds favor it. The significance: If you finance your home with an adjustable loan, there's a likelihood your payments will rise in the future. For this reason, opt for a fixed rate loan. It's true, of course, your initial rate will be higher, but if you can handle a 15-year fully amortized loan, you'll come close to getting the best of both worlds.

4. Don't stint on the down payment. Home purchases can often be financed with small down payments. There's temptation for many buyers to lever into as expensive a home as they can with the least cash possible. I recommend against this for a variety of reasons, but which, if you harbor any caution at all, you can feel in your bones. However, there's a specific minimum down payment to aim for. It's 20 percent, and there's a reason. Loans not exceeding 80 percent of a home's value normally carry lower interest rates, and are exempt from mortgage insurance that adds a premium of about ½ percent per year.

5. Make sure your title is secure and adequate. A form of insurance protection a buyer receives is called *title insurance*. The company providing it examines the ownership record of the property and insures the buyer against any title defects. The premium for this coverage is paid at the time of sale and protects the buyer for as long as ownership lasts. Normally the amount of the coverage is the purchase price, but it's not a bad idea to anticipate the future. As real estate has a tendency to appreciate in value over time, you might consider increasing the face amount of coverage as an added protection. In some states this increase is possible on payment of an additional premium.

6. Hold title wisely. Married couples traditionally hold title to their homes in *joint tenancy*. The reason why is understandable. In the event of a death, the surviving spouse receives automatic title to the property without the inconvenience of probate. Although this solves one problem, there is an inherent disadvantage. Only half the property takes a stepped up basis as of date of death. The other half remains at the original acquisition basis. Under certain circumstances this might result in the imposition of an eventual capital gains tax. This problem is resolved if title is held, instead, as *community property*, where the full property takes the stepped up basis. Check this with your counsel.

7. Be slow to remodel. Now, as you're sitting in your very own home, you see all the things you want to change. To this I say: Certain items of repair may be required at once for simple habitability, but except for these, go slowly. It's best you live in a structure for awhile to get a feel of what you really want. Very simply, a home will grow on you with time, and ideas concocted during your first week of occupancy often seem outlandish by the third month. It's best you spend the first six months in planning, measuring, sketching, collecting prices, inspecting other homes and models, and enthusiastically fantasizing. At the end of that time you may be ready to proceed.

There is, of course, far more to the subject of real estate than its initial acquisition. Of the many books dealing with the countless aspects of real estate ownership, one is truly unique. It is *How I Turned $1,000 into a Million in Real Estate—in my Spare Time*, by William Nickerson. For information on this book, visit my website, www.onthemoneytrail.com, and link on to *Suggested Reading*.

14

HOW TO INSTILL RESPONSIBILITY IN YOUR OFFSPRING

Personal satisfaction comes from earned success, not from handouts. Spoiled children end up dissatisfied, even if they get everything they want. They know deep down they didn't earn it.

A few months ago a subscriber to my newsletter posed a question that, though short and to the point, set me aback. It said: "How far should parents go in helping their financially irresponsible son and wife, with 3 kids? I'm totally frustrated and can't seem to let go because of the grandkids. My son has had a steady job for years making over $50K a year, but their credit is destroyed and they can barely afford a place to live. Thanks." After a few days I cobbled together a reply of sorts, stressing the importance of financial responsibility, the virtues of thrift, and the sanctity of family values. Looking back now on what I said, it's clear my response mouthed all the appropriate pieties, but did not contain one word of practical value. The writer wanted recommendations on how to resolve a pressing problem, and I really didn't have a clue.

Now, after awhile to think about it, I better understand the inadequacy of my reply. The problem posed does not lend itself to resolution. Although the predicament may appear to deal with money—or the lack of it—it's not inherently a financial dilemma. It actually goes far deeper and is the result of a lifetime of behavior which failed to be addressed a quarter century earlier. More to the point, attempting to instill principles or inculcate habits in progeny by their third or fourth decade on this earth will prove to be a futile exercise. It's my belief a person's attitudes and values are pretty well established by the end of puberty. So, let me provide a few guidelines that may help you guide your offspring in more suitable directions.

1. Instruct by Precept and Example. Whether you believe it or not, your children really pay attention to what you say and do. As the first authority normally appearing, a parent becomes a model on which the child fixates. Even before verbal communication is established, parental activities provide guidelines offspring tend instinctively to emulate. Through repetition, later supplemented with oral reinforcement, a bond of behavior develops that can become an ingrained pattern. It's important to realize, however, this input must be consistent if the lessons are to be learned. Thus, if the messages are contradictory, they'll be received as mixed signals by the progeny. If, for example, parents proclaim the importance of living within their financial means while simultaneously indebting themselves through purchases they cannot afford, it won't go undetected by the children nor induce them to pursue habits of thrift. The only way sound financial values can be transmitted from one generation to the next is by a systematic and continuous program that reinforces these values. Only through precept and example will such habits be engrained.

2.   Don't Encourage Unattainable Goals.
Although I regard myself as an optimist, I try to be a realist.
Often parental aspirations fail to keep things in perspective.
Well-meaning parents, who urge their children to *aim for
the stars* while ignoring reality, do them no service. One
typical example is the encouragement given to attend a
prestigious university when family funds are insufficient.
Over the past several years I've fielded many a letter from
these *children*, themselves well into parenthood and
overburdened with tens of thousands of dollars in unpaid
student loans.   In most cases, the grandiose plans
envisioned never came to pass. Whatever added luster a
high-priced school is designed to impart generally proves to
be illusion. Instead, two years at a community college
followed by two more at a local state university, in keeping
with my blueprint of *college on the cheap*, proves far more
appropriate. The value I want to stress is one of realistic
and attainable goals, taking into consideration the inherent
abilities and limitations of each offspring, and this must be
the basis on which guidance is given. Despite the prevalent
attitude in modern society that everyone is endowed to
achieve at any level, the astute parent will recognize when
this is not so and seek to counsel the child accordingly.

3.   Don't Fight Against Human Nature.   We
individuals are programmed to behave in certain ways. Just
as night inexorably follows day, we may expect certain
human actions to trigger other actions. As one example,
it's now established, perhaps not unexpectedly, that if a
high school student is rewarded for report card grades, with
perhaps $100 for each "A" and $50 for each "B," the
student's grades will rise. The anticipated reward triggers
self-interest, with a desire to collect the money as the
primary motive.   From the student's perspective, any
learning acquired that may in the long run prove beneficial

is probably unimportant. What counts is cash in hand. Over the years I've witnessed a lot of strange behavior that ignored human nature. One of the more bizarre instances concerned an overindulged woman in her thirties, who for many years repeatedly received instruction from her wealthy father on how to balance her checkbook. She habitually issued checks whenever she chose. If the account balance fell below zero, the bank phoned her father who deposited more money in the account. Somehow her father never understood his instruction sessions ignored human nature; as the checks always cleared, the checkbook balance held no meaning for her. So what's the purpose of this lesson? It's to stress the importance of parents' awareness of what is important to their offspring. Human nature dictates that all actions actually have meaning.

I'll conclude this subject with a final thought. I firmly believe all actions must have appropriate repercussions. If a youngster is repeatedly sheltered from the adverse effects of bad decisions, there's no reason he or she need contemplate changing the bad behavior. The problem for the parent, of course, is determining what an *appropriate repercussion* shall be. Sorry, but this is as far as I'm able to go. It will be up to each of you parents, on a case by case basis, to figure out what to do. Good luck!

15

TWENTY-FIRST CENTURY THRIFT AND BANKING

*"I rob banks for a living. I consider myself
on a higher moral level than the
crooks who run those banks."*
Willie Sutton

At a local restaurant one evening I received a dramatic lesson in Twenty-first Century banking. My personal credit card was rejected as *nonprocessable*. A prompt phone call to the card issuer, Citibank, revealed the reason: their receipt of a report from the credit agency Experian in which derogatory information showed up on my record. My previous credit limit of $12,900 summarily became $750, and as the card's current balance payable exceeded that sum, it ceased to be usable.

The credit report I obtained through my personal banker the next morning told the story. A mortgage loan payment on an apartment complex I own had been overlooked by my property management firm four months earlier. Upon discovery of the oversight, my manager tendered payment along with the following month's installment. The loan servicer, a major banking entity, reported a "30-day late" to Experian, resulting in reduction of my FICO score from 815 to 726, and triggering the notification to Citibank which effectively cancelled my card. Despite a 7-year record with Citibank, where each month I paid my card balance in full within 48 hours of receipt of the statement, I nonetheless found myself relegated to the status of an undesirable.

In criticizing Citibank's seemingly unwarranted action despite my exemplary payment record, I may be missing the point. Perhaps a more accurate explanation for their conduct is *because of* my exemplary payment record. In an earlier age, banks viewed their best customers as the ones who scrupulously honored their debts by paying on time and incurring no blemishes. In those days the banking industry operated under the *Rule of Three*: pay 3% interest to depositors; charge 3% higher, or 6%, on loans; and be on the golf course by 3 PM. Preferred customers caused no inconvenience. Somewhere along the line bankers discovered a potential bonanza slipping through their fingers. The real profit to be harvested is not the modest interest differential between borrowers and depositors which historically financed the industry, but rather penalties and fees to be imposed. Once that revelation sunk in, banking officials became obsessed with setting rules to maximize profit, and nothing matched the potential of imposing punitive interest rates whenever possible. I recognize now Citibank regards me as unprofitable and expendable. Over my years as a cardholder they've yet to collect a dime in interest, late charges, or fees of any sort. If their actions induce me to close my account in disgust, it will probably cause them to rejoice.

The public's attitude toward thrift is far different than in an earlier era. It's a rare event when someone systematically saves up to purchase for cash such things as furniture, a computer, or an automobile. The accepted procedure is to arrange a time account, often on a credit card, for which interest at some rate must be paid if the cardholder chooses to pay less than the full card balance each month. It is this rate, set unilaterally by the card issuer that can easily defy logic. Clearly, their aim is the maximum the traffic will bear. To attract business, banks regularly solicit credit card customers by offering low interest rates on transfer balances from the accounts of competing lenders. Here's the pitch Citibank used: "Dear Mr. Jacobs, Because of your good standing, you are pre-approved to apply for our Citi® Diamond Preferred® Card with low APR on balance transfers. There's no annual fee and no balance transfer fee with this offer." The accompanying letter prominently boasts "0% APR" for 12 months, followed by a rate of 8.24% thereafter. Less noticeable on the reverse side, in far finer print, you will find the *qualifiers*. "We can change the rates, fees, and terms of your account at any time for any reasons . . . such as your failure to make payments to another creditor when due. All your APRs may automatically increase up to the Default APR if you default under any . . . " and on and on it goes. Not so incidentally, the Default APR listed is 29.74%. It takes no imagination to understand how the game is rigged. Prospective customers are lured with giveaway interest rates, only to be nailed to the cross as soon as something—almost anything—can be rationalized as "a reason" to automatically increase the rate. This variation on a traditional bait and switch tactic must be devastating on those poor unfortunates unable to pay their full card balance each month.

What I fail to understand is why the general public ever allowed itself to accept the concept that an increasingly higher level of personal debt is acceptable.

How can someone with limited income permit a portion of their income to evaporate as interest? Nonetheless, an increasingly high level of debt is now accepted as customary by a substantial portion of the American public. In a report by the Federal Reserve, consumer credit rose at an annual rate of 5.9 percent in July 2013, lead by an 8.1 percent increase in revolving credit, the category including credit card loans. Apparently consumers are using their cards more to finance purchases now that home equity lines of credit are less available. Perhaps the public's increased tendency to go into hock can be attributed to the power of advertising, which is one more concept I fail to understand.

Let me conclude with a personal observation. Any organization employing the sort of highhanded tactics just described is one from which we are all better off keeping a safe distance. I will, possibly, terminate my account should I obtain a new MasterCard through my local bank. As I suggested earlier, Citibank will be as pleased to be rid of me as I will of them.

16

RANDOM THOUGHTS ON THE ROAD TO PROSPERITY

*The real test of your character
is what it takes to stop you.*

As you navigate the Road to Prosperity, you'll come into contact with a lot of persons and institutions with which you must figuratively engage in mortal combat if you're to survive. Recognize from the onset the financial world does not resemble Shangri La, nor do the many entrepreneurs, representatives and agents you'll encounter necessarily mean you well. It's said, with some accuracy, the one guiding principle on which you may rely in your dealings is:

It's every rat for himself!

With that as a lead-in, I'll now pass on several revelations I learned the hard way.

Dealing with Financial Advisors. Only the rare citizen has an ability to invest wisely. This takes a talent few possess. So, with billions of investment dollars in the hands of Americans, professional investment advisors occupy a position of prominence. Unfortunately, many practitioners who offer their advisory services are equally devoid of investment expertise. The result is predictable; huge sums are woefully misdirected. To protect yourself, you may try to prequalify your counselor. However, don't expect credentials, such as certification, will ensure proficiency. Comedian Mel Brooks once provided this classic definition of *certified*: "You're a nice guy . . . we like you . . . you're certified." Understand, as with many other products, financial planning is an exercise in pure marketing. You've seen the newspaper and television advertisements guaranteeing each client will prosper. A sense of skepticism suggests the persons who write the ads are unrelated to those who recommend the investments. A final warning: You cannot depend upon a hired advisor to responsibly invest your money. You must develop an understanding of what constitutes an acceptable investment so the final decisions are yours.

Dealing with your Banker. Over the past decade or so, banking officials made a fascinating discovery. They found their customers to be an untapped source of bounty, with depositors willing to accept minuscule interest on their savings while tolerating the payment of fees and assessments limited only by the imagination of the bank hierarchy. Now, in the sixth year of what appears to be a prolonged slump, interest rates paid on bank savings accounts can be seen as low as one-tenth of one percent annually. However, those ultra-low rates are not reflected in the charges your bank may impose for any variety of "services." Should you issue a check for one dollar over your account balance, or pay your credit card bill one day later than the deadline date, you'll be slapped with a penalty which can calculate out to annual percentage rates of twenty percent or higher. My advice: Regularly scrutinize your bank statements to see what might be slipped in. Only your active participation will protect you.

Dealing with Government. The most frightening words you will ever hear are: "Hello, I'm from the government, and I'm here to help you." Let's wade into the center of what government is all about. It can be summed up in one word: *Taxes*. And don't be confused when you're hit with a *surcharge* or a *statutory penalty*. As far as the tax collector is concerned, it's just another tax . . . as the following several lines explain.

> Call it *duty*, *charge* or *fee*.
> Makes no difference, wait and see.
> You will surely find the same,
> *tax* by any other name,
>   smells as sweet,
>   cuts as deep.

Left to the devices of the officials, there's no limit to the amount to be collected, and any attempt by the payors to minimize the tribute will be met with the usual warnings of consequences which never end. It's for this reason you must be cautious in your dealings with government. Do not fail to respond to notices from them. Do not accept their offer to calculate your income taxes. Keep records of all contacts with officials. And above all, never entertain any doubts about what the government wants from you. It wants your money.

◆   ◆   ◆

This seems to be a good time to caution you as to three particularly bad ways to spend money. For those of you who resent being told what *not* to do, I'll do a switch-hit and paint a pleasing picture of some deplorable ways to blow your dough.

The pricey nuptial is just the thing. A simple wedding, where the bride and groom exchange vows in the presence of family and friends, then adjourn to a garden or chapel anteroom for light refreshments, will never do. It's simply too plebian. What you really want is pizzazz. This means elegant clothing, ostentatious display, a large banquet hall, expensive floral arrangements and party favors, the finest cuisine for no less than 300 guests, a 15-piece band, and all topped off with a 2-week honeymoon to some exotic place in a 4-figure-per-night bridal suite. This is what tying the knot is all about. And whether the marriage lasts through the season is immaterial. What really counts is blowing the dough in a way to make everyone envious.

The only way to go! Death is the one event none of us will avoid; no one gets to opt out of that experience. But the final sendoff is another story, with a bevy of choices available. The average cost of a funeral in the United States today, excluding the cemetery expenses, is just over $5,500, of which 42% represents the casket price. However, an increasing number of funerals, currently 28%, incorporate last rites with less expensive cremation, this option up from only 5% three decades ago. An even more economic alternative is through an affiliate of a funeral society, where the recently departed can be cremated and the last remains disposed of for less than $800. Any desired memorial service can easily be postponed until a later date, a mortician's contrary opinion notwithstanding. Unfortunately, our problem with a dignified low cost funeral is fundamental; we don't get to spend much. What you really want is a gala celebration, in obvious poor taste, that can set you back tens of thousands of dollars. This, then, allows the dearly departed to take satisfaction while viewing the festivities from up above—or perhaps from down below.

The waste of last resort. Is it possible your assets persist, despite your best efforts to rid yourself of unwanted cash? Then your efforts must be directed toward the last frontier: the gambling arena. Luckily there's no shortage of routes you may take to be regally fleeced. Be it Pimlico, Belmont Park, Churchill Downs, or elsewhere, the horses are always running. It's said, in every race someone wins. That's certainly true, though what's ignored is the only *consistent* winner is the pari-mutuel system. But if the nags are not to your liking, there's surely a lottery near you. Currently 29 states and the District of Columbia operate government lotteries, with billions of dollars generated annually. And as expected, the officials operate a sure thing. The income and payouts are regulated to make certain the player loses. And finally, if all else fails, there's the casino. At an earlier time it required effort to respond to the lure of Las Vegas or Atlantic City, but no more. Over half the nation's states together with several Canadian provinces now host Indian casinos, where roulette wheels, blackjack tables, and slot machines operate around-the-clock to scalp the paleface—and whoever else strays onto the reservation. I'm afraid it's too late to circle the wagons, as most of them already have chattel mortgages attached.

Send your offspring to the finest universities. The fact learning can be acquired inexpensively is no reason not to expend huge sums in its attainment. With tuition, books, fees, lodging, and incidentals included, you should be able to blow upwards of $40,000 annually for each child if the right schools are chosen. You may have heard two years at a community college, followed by two years at a local state university commuting from home, can provide a motivated student with as fine an education as four years in residence at Harvard or Princeton. Despite the fact this is true, it won't meet your basic requirement: getting rid of the money you don't want. Therefore, you know what you must do. Encourage each of your offspring to select a high-priced institution at an exclusive location. It may not address their needs, but it will resolve your problem.

Never say no! Did your brother-in-law just lose his weekly paycheck by a bad pick on the third race at Hialeah? If he needs a bit to tide him over, give him your help. Is a generous contribution to the bridal shower of your coworker's daughter requested? It will certainly be a nice gesture on your part. The plea given from the pulpit by your pastor last Sunday made it clear; without your assistance, the natives of Rwanda will continue to suffer. Surely you can't turn your back on mankind. And as there is no limit to the needs others will impose on you, it's a reliable device to rid yourself of money. Simply turn off your head and follow your heart

Accept your stockbroker's advice without question. Should a heavily loaded mutual fund be recommended, as it most assuredly will, signify your approval with a nod of the head and a broad smile. Finally, as a last resort, if your portfolio refuses to head in a sufficiently southward direction, give discretionary authority to your stockbroker. In this way, the inevitable churning of your account to generate maximum commissions for the broker, irrespective of performance, will be guaranteed. Simply follow this program and you may be certain you'll not find yourself buried in unwanted profits nor deluged with unmanageable assets that you don't know what to do with. Quite to the contrary, you may rest assured your status as a working stiff will be guaranteed into perpetuity.

17

SECOND THOUGHTS ON INVESTING

Don't expect much worthwhile advice from securities analysts. If they really knew anything, they probably wouldn't tell you anyway.

This article is directed to the quintessential American investor. Even though I don't know you personally, I can predict what your investments consist of. Except for your home, the majority of your assets are held as shares in open-end investment companies, commonly known as mutual funds. On the whole, most will be equity funds, with many of them index-based. If you're past the mid-century mark, you'll possess some balanced funds, so interest-bearing securities such as corporate or U.S. treasury bonds comprise a portion of the mix. And for the more aggressive among you, a portion of those funds will be marginally exotic, including holdings backed by such things as precious metals, Ginnie Mae mortgages, and the international sector, or perhaps some hedge funds. But, basic to it all, and predicated purely on faith, the fortunes of most Americans are today controlled by a host of nameless and faceless persons who administer the thousand of funds dominating the world of corporate securities.

How can it be, in a society as diverse and highly educated as ours, the vast majority of citizens relegate their financial futures to a labyrinth over which they have little understanding or control? The reason is fundamental. It's because the average person knows relatively little about handling assets. Whatever praise or criticism you may direct at the American public school system, one thing must be acknowledged: The handling of personal financial affairs is not a subject to which much attention is devoted. Whatever the average American knows about investing money did not come from the classroom. This is understandable, of course, if only because the typical classroom teacher is equally mystified by the world of money. So, with a vacuum to be filled, it's only reasonable an industry developed to profit from the public's dearth of expertise. And make no mistake, the mutual fund industry is profitable—highly so. With such contrivances as sales charges, deferred loads, redemption fees, reinvestment loads, 12b-1 plan charges, and management fees, a substantial percentage of investors' potential return is filtered off annually. It's my belief the principal reason mutual funds exist is for collection of fees by the operators. Everything else is peripheral.

For those of you who concur—perhaps grudgingly—with my analysis of mutual fund limitations, perhaps it's time you begin to tailor your investment program a little more selectively. If your preference is for corporate securities, you might consider choosing your own stocks and bonds. Thanks to modern technology, the concept of a separately managed account is no longer the exclusive province for the ultra-wealthy. With total assets no greater than $100,000, it's possible to obtain an institutional money manager to handle your account at a flat annual charge of about 2 percent of total assets, and this includes all advisory fees, commissions, money management, and administrative costs. What you will accomplish is to create a sort of individual mini-mutual fund operating without the expenses and hidden fees which often bring the annual charges of a traditional mutual fund substantially higher.

Admittedly, if you intend to self-direct your investment portfolio, you must begin to actually analyze the securities you buy and sell, rather than leave it to the discretion of mutual fund managers. Although initially you may not feel competent to handle the task, the likelihood is after a little selective investigation, you'll be up to it. As a preliminary exercise, there's a book you must read. It's *The Intelligent Investor*, by Benjamin Graham. Although this 640-page work dates back to 1949, its most recent 2006 edition, available at Amazon, is as current as if written today. It will give you the information you'll need to fathom the securities market. If you're inclined to devote a little more time to the preliminaries, there's a second helpful publication: *The Simple Strategy for Successful Investing in Only 15 Minutes a Week!*, by Phil Town. Published in 2006 by Crown, these 320 pages should fill in any mental blank spaces Mr. Graham may have omitted. Having thus established a firm foundation, together with a subscription to *Wall Street Journal*, and perhaps to *Barron's*, you'll do a far finer job handling your assets than the average mutual fund manager.

Before I conclude this dissertation, there's one more factor deserving consideration. By referring back a couple of paragraphs ago, you'll find a sentence that begins: "If your preference is for corporate securities…" At this point I want to make it clear that far more investment opportunities exist than merely corporate securities. There's a world of real estate under our feet, and for those persons willing to immerse themselves in the medium, there are fortunes to be made. Furthermore, lending money provides excellent opportunities. When witnessing the effects of compound interest over a sufficient period of time, returns can prove most rewarding. Finally, investment-like business opportunities present themselves from time to time. For the knowledgeable individual with an eye toward reward, these can sometimes appear as manna from heaven. It's my recommendation you not limit yourself to a single type of investment. In furtherance of that goal, I invite you to visit my website at www.onthemoneytrail.com and click onto *Newsletter Archives*, where you'll find a variety of articles on all sorts of financial matters. If scanning these writings does nothing more than whet your appetite for additional information, it will have served its purpose.

18

THAR'S GOLD IN THEM THAR BONDS

Interest is not something you pay.
It is something you earn.

Corporate bonds conjure up images of the past—sometimes not attractive. Even today a favorite slur on the affluent includes references to *coupon clippers*, depicting greedy men somehow in the process of reaping the rewards of the labor of others while performing no productive function for society. Probably many of the persons making such accusations don't know what "coupon clipping" is or, rather, *was*. So *you* don't run this risk, let me explain. In earlier times, mostly before World War II, corporations and municipalities borrowed money from the public by issuing unregistered bonds known as "bearer bonds." They redeemed at maturity in the face amount of the bond.

The interest, normally payable in semiannual installments and evidenced by coupons attached, traded for cash by delivery either directly to the company or to any commercial bank. As each coupon became due, the holder "clipped" it off with scissors and submitted for payment. The corporation made no attempt to keep a record of the owners of these bonds; whoever presented the coupons or the matured certificate received the cash—no questions asked.

With the passage of years, corporations ceased doing business in this manner. Near the end of their time, bearer bonds became a favorite of tax evaders seeking to avoid reporting interest income. As expected, the government legislated them out of existence. Bonds in use today are registered to the holder, and the corporation makes an annual report to the tax collector of the interest paid.

Though interest-bearing securities such as corporate bonds and treasury obligations are regarded as the investment for the rich and sedentary, it's my belief they belong in any growing estate, and the sooner, the better. What occurs is a multiplying effect which, over time, is little short of phenomenal. It's said someone once asked Thomas Edison, in his later years, to identify mankind's greatest invention. His response: "compound interest." Whether the tale is true is of little importance. What really matters are the actual results of a series of investments, at a predetermined rate of interest, over a prolonged period. An excellent application of this principle would be in a tax-deferred retirement program such as an Individual Retirement Account (IRA), or better yet, a tax-exempt Roth IRA.

Before we begin a more detailed analysis of specific bonds, you are entitled to a few suggestions. Above all, don't actually buy anything until you understand what you're doing. This means you must expend time and effort to read up on the subject. A number of good books on bonds exist. One of the more scholastic is Christina I. Ray's *The Bond Market, Trading and Risk Management.*

Though keenly analytic and absolutely thorough, perhaps to the point of pedantry, it is hard to justify its high price. For your purposes, either of two less expensive books will do the job nicely. One, published by the New York Institute of Finance, is Robert Zipf's *How the Bond Market Works*. The other is Sharon Saltzgiver Wright's *Getting Started in Bonds*. Perhaps not surprisingly, the information provided is remarkably similar to what I learned a quarter century ago. My introductory bond expertise came from two publications: Hugh C. Sherwood, *How to Invest in Bonds*, 1974, and Eliot Janeway, *You and Your Money*, 1972, which sold for $2.95 and $5.95 respectively. They might do the job satisfactorily today, but are most likely long out of print.

This brings us to specific recommendations. When selecting bonds, consider the following:

A.   Deal with a brokerage firm, whether conventional or on the web, that offers a broad selection of company-owned or controlled bonds which can be purchased from their daily generated lists at a net price to you. This is preferable to chasing bonds on the open market. Merrill Lynch and Charles Schwab are two such firms, among many others.

B.   Deal exclusively in corporate bonds of major public companies, preferably those listed on the New York Stock Exchange (NYSE). Avoid the municipal (muni) bond market, despite the tax avoidance benefits they offer, and irrespective of high ratings certain municipal bond issues may enjoy. The likelihood bond-issuing governmental agencies may work hand in glove with courts and regulatory bodies to defraud bondholders in difficult financial times, seems more than a vague possibility.

Just such an event occurred in 1983 when the Washington State Supreme Court ruled eighty-eight public utilities companies need not honor contracts to buy electrical power from the Washington Public Power Supply System (WPPSS). The event, since referred to as the "WHOOPS debacle," related to defaulted bonds backed by terminated nuclear power projects. Although confronted with inherently unchallengeable contracts, and despite partial guarantees by the Bonneville Power Administration, a federal agency, the court declared them invalid. In this way, they ruled for the benefit of the local voting utility-users at the expense of mostly out-of-state bondholders who lost millions, casting doubts on the stability of *all* municipal bonds.

For a follow-up lesson on this subject, *fast-forward* to Tuesday, December 6, 1994, when prosperous Orange County, California, filed under Chapter Nine of the bankruptcy code, throwing into question $1.5 billion of the county's bonds. Prior to that date they received top ratings from both S&P and Moody's despite growing public evidence of accumulating market losses. The political maneuverings over the following eighteen months did little to assure bondholders. As to both WHOOPS and Orange County, do not think such circumstances cannot occur again.

      C. Select bonds with maturities in the range of two to five years. Though you may receive somewhat lower interest than with longer-term bonds, you protect yourself from fluctuation due to changing interest rates. In addition, by holding your bonds this relatively short period to full maturity, you avoid marketing them through a stockbroker, thus saving a commission on the sale

.

Of course by avoiding long-term bonds, you give up the possibility a rapid drop in interest rates provides a substantial increase in bond value and, with it, a fortuitous capital gain. This, however, is one of the drawbacks of an admittedly stodgy investment. But if what you seek in your bond investment program is inspiring innovation—perhaps better described as hopeful speculation—look elsewhere. You will find no encouragement here.

D.   Avoid bond funds; they offer nothing you cannot do better yourself. The "diversification" benefit of a fund over even small purchases of bonds is minimal if you choose your bonds with care. As to the debate over *load funds* versus *no load funds*, be assured the load is there somewhere. The primary reason brokerage firms prefer funds over individual bond purchases is that commission per invested dollar is far greater, sometimes as much as fivefold.

E.   Try to select bonds which can be purchased at discount or, at most, par. If a premium must be paid for the bond, make certain its terms provide it cannot be called (paid off) by the issuing company early at a price less than your purchase price.   If you ignore this, you may experience *yield to call* being far less favorable than your anticipated *yield to maturity*.

F.   Despite my quarrel with the rating services, avoid bonds with an S&P rating below BBB (known as *investment grade*). The one exception to this rule might be a bond rated BB+ which appears otherwise to meet the criteria for soundness. The particular advantage is that, with its failure to qualify as investment grade, it's excluded from many portfolios, and may be priced to attain a disproportionately higher yield. With this sole exception, however, it probably pays to aim for the BBB and A ratings. However, avoid bonds rated AA and AAA, if only because their perceived higher security translates to an inflated price and, correspondingly, a lower yield. The extra safety represented by these more highly rated bonds does not justify the extra price you pay for them.

I'll offer a final caution to you before you begin your bond investment program. From the onset you will receive advice from many sources cautioning you corporate bonds are not the way to go. You'll be told equity securities, either stocks or stock funds, are superior in every way, that bonds will not enable you to keep up with inflation, and neither income flow nor long term appreciation is favored by bond investment. Be aware this advice will come regularly from those persons who aim to sell investments to you. And understand the fees and commissions to be received by these advisors will be considerably reduced by your acquisition of bonds as I've outlined here. Keep this in mind as you pursue your investment program.

19

MARKETING IN AMERICA: HOW DID IT COME TO THIS?

"No one ever went broke underestimating
the taste of the American public."
H. L. Mencken

Growing to maturity during the first half of the twentieth century, I experienced my share of marketing. With radio as the predominant medium, singing commercials filled the airwaves. Many were memorable, with a few truly enjoyable. My favorite jingle went like this:

> Pepsi Cola hits the spot
> Twelve full ounces, that's a lot
> Twice as much for a nickel too
> Pepsi Cola is the drink for you

Those four delightful lines caressed my ear until 1958, and sold a lot of Pepsi. Here's another catchy ad that found favor with the buying public:

Use Ajax, the foaming cleanser
Cleans your sink just like a whiz
You'll stop paying the elbow tax
When you start cleaning with Ajax
So use Ajax, the foaming cleanser
Floats the dirt right down the drain

The popularity of that little ditty enabled the product to outsell its chief rival, Old Dutch Cleanser. Other such commercials, usually forgettable, appeared and disappeared over the years, but even the most insipid seemed tolerable. Advertisers at the time recognized a need for some rationality. Even though the snake oil salesman prevailed as an American tradition, those willing to believe outrageous claims remained relegated to the gullible fringes of society.

Things are different today. The fare appearing regularly on radio and television reveals nothing to be beyond the pale. On any day, paying only the slightest attention to the media, you will discover the following:

• You can turn debt into wealth. Regardless of your income, credit rating, or amount of obligations, you can become fabulously wealthy in a matter of months, enabling you to live a life of luxury on the French Riviera. A simple phone call to the listed number will arrange this.

• A prominent auto manufacturer believes you will be enticed to purchase its vehicle by viewing it swerving around death-defying curves on a narrow mountain road at 90 miles per hour.

• One of the nation's leading lending institutions offers assurance you need pay no more than 3¼ percent annually for a 30-year, fixed-rate home loan, with no other costs involved. However, the annual percentage rate on that payday loan you floated last week amounts to 76.8 percent. Is there some dichotomy at work that's not apparent?

• A well-known Southern California casino wants to reward you with the "winningest slots," suggesting the odds are with you. It's an offer you can't refuse, delivered at 420 words per minute at a 130-decibel sound level.

• Are you embarrassed because your schooling never extended beyond 9th grade? No problem! Within a month you too can become a college graduate. Receive a Bachelor's Degree, or Master's . . . or even a Doctorate. A well-publicized institution will reward "your life's experience" by bestowing upon you, for a fee, the diploma to which you're entitled. Send for the brochure today and obtain your "passport to success" tomorrow.

These are but a sample of the nostrums spewed regularly, lending credence to the skeptic's adage that *ninety-five percent of everything is nonsense.* Can it be a substantial portion of the consuming public fails to recognize these pitches as patently absurd? But more to the point, relative to marketing in America, I'll re-ask the question of this article's title: *How Did It Come To This?* It appears an entire industry functions on transparent deception. Is it because there's something uniquely lacking in our collective good sense? I'll concede I'm without an answer to that question.

The question which *is* answerable is far more fundamental. Does an outpouring of hyperbole actually sell product? It appears the answer is *yes*, for firms engaging in these sorts of sales practices show consistent profits year after year. Most of the nation's major banks, peddling credit cards with interest rates often in excess of 30 percent annually, do not lack customers. Gambling houses and state lotteries now permeate the landscape, with each offering itself as the road to riches. Insurance companies which foist off annuities and real estate firms that hawk timeshare projects are but two more examples of the successful promotion of high mark-up merchandise. What can be stated unequivocally is that a substantial portion of the buying public is willing to ignore all rationality as it responds to sales appeals which defy logic. It's clear, regardless of the reasons, duplicitous marketing is remarkably effective.

I'll sum things up for you. It's a hostile world in which we live, and commercial enterprises with products for sale will use every device at their command to push those wares. To survive with your purse or billfold intact requires you display skepticism in your dealings. If a presentation does not make complete sense, reject it. If an assertion seems unwarranted, ignore it. If you feel under pressure to commit to anything with which you're uncomfortable, extricate yourself as quickly as possible. Remember always, marketers of products are not your friends, nor will they further your best interests. If the representation of a commodity seems illogical, avoid it like the plague.

20

IS SOCIAL SECURITY A GIGANTIC PONZI SCHEME?

Welcome to the Social Security system: deceptively designed and fraudulently administered. It could not otherwise function.

Before I offer any predictions for the future of the Social Security system, let me relate an historical tale. It may seem unrelated, but bear with me—there *is* a relevance. The story involves an Italian citizen, born in 1882, who immigrated as a young man to Boston, Massachusetts, by way of Canada. His occupations during his life included grocery salesman, sewing machine repairman, cafe waiter, and hot dog stand operator. After several prison terms and eventual deportation, he ended his days in Brazil, dying near-penniless in a Rio de Janeiro charity ward in 1949. He receives but minor mention in encyclopedias, and relatively few accounts exist which document his life on earth. However, for one short period from December 1919 to August 1920, he personified

success.   His name: Charles Ponzi.   His claim to
immortality: the *Ponzi Scheme*.

On the pretext of capitalizing on international
exchange rate differentials through trading in postal reply
coupons, he claimed to obtain annual returns far in excess
of 100 percent. On this basis he sold short-term notes to
the public, offering as much as 50 percent interest in as
little as forty-five days. By systematically paying off
earlier note purchasers with receipts from later customers,
he rapidly developed for many Bostonians an image of
authenticity and reliability. Within a scant six months he
collected eight million dollars from speculators eager for
the promised rewards—a prodigious sum at the time.
Though not the first person to engineer such a scam, he
qualified as the most colorful. Not unexpectedly, when the
investors ultimately began to doubt his ability to honor the
note commitments, his financial collapse promptly
followed, with imprisonment not long afterward.

We'll now return to the social security system and
the logical question: Are there any lessons to be learned
when contrasting its operation with the financial empire of
Charles Ponzi?   Certain comparisons seem obvious,
specifically that money is collected today to pay sums to
those who decades ago paid significantly lesser amounts.
However, this fact in itself does not necessarily signal a
calamitous end to the program.   Regardless of the
similarities, there are two notable differences. In the first
place, Social Security together with its Medicare
companion, function legally under the direction, and with
the full blessing, of the federal government. Though it will
encounter political challenges, and be forced to
accommodate to changing tastes and national
temperaments, conceivably it can continue as long as the
United States government is itself viable. Secondly, and of

equal importance, short of actual citizen revolt it will not lose its source of funding since contributions are mandatory, not voluntary.

In case you're unaware of the financial conditions of Social Security, you might note that in 2010 the previously cash-producing system ran a $49 billion deficit by spending more than it took in. For those of you who plan to rely upon the government's assurance of *long-term solvency of Social Security*, you must delve a little more closely into the administrators' reports. Government actuaries have determined the $2.7 trillion trust fund, which ensures the system, will be exhausted by 2033 as expenditures regularly exceed income. Does this suggest future recipients may not enjoy the sort of benefits current recipients receive? I'll risk the government's displeasure and offer a prediction on Social Security's future. Let's fast-forward a few years as millions more retiring baby boomers swell the system's ranks. With anticipated payments exceeding collections and general insolvency forecast for 2033, will the government actually allow the system to generate an outpouring of red ink which would bankrupt the nation? It's my belief no administration will permit economic destruction of the nation merely to maintain an economically unfeasible illusion. Something must give!

Now that I've revealed what will not happen to social security, you're entitled to know what will happen. Regardless of philosophic inclination or party affiliation of persons elected to executive and legislative office, there's really not much choice. An economically unsustainable agenda cannot continue indefinitely. At some point it must either become viable or self-destruct. And that is what it will become—viable. As the money runs out, contributions will rise and benefits will shrink. There is, of course, a practical limit beyond which the FICA tax may not extend. As with all taxes, the limit is one of "collectability," usually reflecting the point when political considerations overrule the attempt to extract further revenue. The matter of shrinking benefits is easier to envision. Expected changes will include full rather than just partial taxability for those above an income threshold. Following will be systematic reductions of those limits until social security benefits become fully taxable to all recipients. The next modifications will be a further increase in the retirement age as a prerequisite for eligibility as well as a reduction in the size of retirement payments to wealthy Americans. This is merely the start.

The major changes will begin when the situation becomes more aggravated. Within a generation *means testing*, and eventually *assets limitation*, will convert it into a system to which all will continue to pay, but only those who qualify as needy will receive benefits. The real pity, of course, is today's young and middle-age, middle-class, middle-income citizens are being bled to death to sustain a fiction from which they will receive, at best, a pittance. For those of you disillusioned with social security, I understand your plight. To watch your FICA tax money pour out in an unending stream is disheartening, particularly as the politicians continue to haggle among themselves over minutiae. We are witnessing business as usual while a bevy of modern day Neros fiddle. But, perhaps the saddest part of all is for the mass of you paying the bill to maintain this sinkhole, there is nothing you can do about it. You will continue to sustain the labyrinth during its transition into the system it will become.

I'll summarize this topic with a troubling prognosis. There is no way the government can avoid the catastrophic collapse in store for Social Security and Medicare. It will ultimately morph into a welfare system to which all will contribute, but from which only the destitute will collect. Whatever you can do to avoid its grasp will be to your individual benefit. Those of you coerced into the system will have no choice but to hope for the best. As with so many other misfortunes flesh is heir to, each of us must fend for ourselves, as best we can.

With that said, let me share this thought: There are those who accuse the government of running Social Security as a Ponzi scheme. This is an insult to the memory of Charles Ponzi. He never forced anyone to subscribe to *his* scam.

As a final offering on this subject, perhaps you'll enjoy the following historical review of Social Security, presented in a way you can visualize.

♦　　♦　　♦　　♦

SECURITY FOR ALL

Have ever you wondered, in moments of trial,
As much of life's course goes askew,
How some trends come in style,
That we can't reconcile,
And why matters turn out as they do?

Some programs evolve much as they are begun,
While others transform as they grow.
But I'll tell you of one,
That before all is done,
Its founders would surely *not* know.

The year—nineteen hundred and thirty five,
A worldwide depression prevailed.
In his African drive,
Mussolini would strive,
To rebuild ancient Rome—but he failed.

And that was the year of the "Long March" by Mao;
Some six thousand miles he did trek.
There was no telling how
His *red book* might avow,
The plain truth of a China he'd wreck.

So it naturally followed in that fateful year,
An event of momentous impact.
A law *all* might cheer—
At the start most austere—
The Social Security Act.

There was fanfare and ritualistic display,
On the fourteenth of August, its birth.
Premonition, you'd say—
On the very next day,
Will Rogers departed this earth.

In the nineteen thirties slim notice was paid,
To the future of what had begun.
Scant collections were made—
Even less was outlaid.
The effect on *most* people was *none*.

The forties and fifties both smiled as they passed,
But with tinkering now here and there.
Full abundance, steadfast—
An economy vast—
The program had money to spare.

Then the nineteen hundred and sixties arrived,
As vulgar deceptions were hatched.
With all caution aside,
LBJ then contrived,
That a Medicare load be attached.

With that it was clear a new pattern evolved,
Though ever so slowly to form.
As restraints were dissolved,
Jurisdiction devolved,
To the groups for which greed was the norm.

No longer would standard restraint be the aim,
Nor fiscal forbearance prevail.
Absolution from blame,
Made indulgence the game—
The dog would be wagged by the tail.

As the seventies dawned it was vividly clear,
That the built-up reserves could not last.
What to do? Have no fear!
They would just commandeer
Some spare fees till the problem had passed.

So the hard-working citizen financed the scheme,
Through the tax known as F–I–C–A.
Though bereft, it would seem,
There was held out the dream,
That it all would be solvent one day.

By the year nineteen hundred and eighty one,
Dire rumors were casting a pall.
A campaign was begun,
And the tale neatly spun,
That no problems existed at all.

But despite the assurances issued on high,
The workingman's quandary grew.
That the plan was awry,
He could well certify,
As he kissed his earnings adieu.

And into the nineties, amidst the travail,
With the tribute each year seen to rise,
Uncle Sam, without fail,
Had a bear by the tail,
And was tied to the enterprise.

The grip on the worker dared not be released.
No leeway existed at all.
The assault never ceased—
Youthful Peter was fleeced,
For the payment to elderly Paul.

So where are we now at this moment in life—
A new century caught in the throes?
Animosities rife—
Generational strife—
And a nation of rancorous foes.

The billions that poured, with no sign of relent,
Now described as the "*Trust Fund*" reserve,
Have all long since been spent,
On farm aid and cheap rent,
And to give the Serbs what they deserve.

And meanwhile our leaders, rejecting all blame,
In a manner which seems most depraved,
Loot the *Fund*, with no shame,
As they proudly proclaim,
That "Social Security's Saved!"

So what will it be in the future someday?
Might the system enjoy a rebirth?
I can think of *one* way:
Hold your breath and just pray.
There's no other chance on this earth.

The moral, if any, I wish to instill,
And I hope, for your sake, that you heed,
Is: No government will
Handle problems with skill,
For they *are* the problem, indeed.

21

INVESTING LIKE A MILLIONAIRE

In this life, one thing counts.
In the bank, large amounts.
From the Broadway musical *Oliver*

The title of a *USA Today* article attracted my attention: "You don't have to be a millionaire to invest like one." The article, by columnist John Waggoner, described sensible mutual fund investment, expounding on such matters as sales and load charges, annual Roth IRA limits, and automatic reinvestment programs. But search as I might, I found no information on how to invest like a millionaire.

It then occurred to me, an article's author seldom selects its title. It's assigned to a newspaper employee, not for describing the column's contents, but for attracting attention. Apparently I was not about to discover secret investment techniques of the wealthy. Perhaps it's just as well, for the mere possession of wealth is no guarantee its holder will invest wisely. Possibly such a thought seems sacrilegious, for the world seems to subscribe to a line from the Broadway musical *Fiddler on the Roof*: "When you're rich, they think you really know."

So said, you're entitled to a glimpse at how millionaires actually invest. Consider no less a person than TV celebrity Larry King who, at one time, filed suit against an insurance brokerage, claiming to have been tricked in a sophisticated insurance sales transaction which proved financially catastrophic. Neither his wealth nor celebrity status prevented the misfortune.

You may add to the list of victims many sports personalities, such as NBA legend Jerry West and Dodgers third-baseman Nomar Garciaparra, who accused their prominent Los Angeles investment advisor of gouging them out of millions of dollars in excessive commissions on bond trades. Admittedly, sports figures are notoriously naïve on monetary matters, but certainly their wealth did not protect them.

Even well-to-do individuals, astute in the ways of Wall Street, are not immune to a swindle. George L. Forbes, one-time President of the Cleveland City Council, who sat on the state commission overseeing hundreds of millions in assets, fell victim to a scam that bilked dozens of wealthy investors out of some $300 million. His financial prowess proved to be no defense.

At this moment I suspect you're likely to say: "Wait a minute! You're talking about rich celebrities who would be natural targets for con artists. What about the *ordinary* millionaires who go about their lives sensibly, conducting their investment programs in the same businesslike manner which made them millionaires in the first place?" Okay, your point is effectively made. There are a certain number of the prosperous among us who perform much as you describe, but the odds are against them. What you must understand is that the investment advisory world is not designed to bestow favorable treatment upon persons merely because they possess high net worth. As a group, wealthy individuals represent nothing more than a source of assets to be tapped. It's true, of course, you'd not know this from the advertisements of the major funds, brokerages, and financial planning firms, which seem instead to stress dedication to each client's best interests. Never forget the public relations staffs drafting those ads operate on a different plane than the departments which actually service clients. Does this suggest the investment industry is actually a cynically-devised marketing scheme? Most certainly! By necessity, all marketing programs must be cynically devised and executed.

If you think I'm overstating things, look closely at the most rapidly growing investment arena of the decade: the hedge fund—a major industry devoted exclusively to romancing the wealthy. Hedge funds, as their name implies, generally seek to offset potential losses in the markets in which they operate by hedging their investments through a variety of complex strategies such as short selling, futures trading, use of leverage, and other techniques. They're aided in this endeavor by being exempt from most securities regulation.

The salient aspect of these funds is they are accessible only to "accredited investors," defined by federal law as persons with a seven-figure net worth or annual income exceeding $200,000. Membership in this august group enables those so favored to partake of special benefits, most notably the payment of fees that could choke a rhinoceros. The customary charge is known as "two and twenty," reflecting an annual *management fee* of 2% of an investor's gross asset value, plus an additional 20% *performance fee*, based upon computed profits, both unrealized and actual, on each investment. However, annual management fees up to 5% and performance fees as high as 44% are not unknown. In addition, these charges are generally collected monthly, or in some cases weekly, which can effectively lock in short term windfall profits for the hedge fund managers.

As expected, the incentive for management to take inordinate risks is more than a remote possibility. This explains why once-prominent Amaranth Advisors, a Connecticut-based hedge fund, slipped down the drain along with $6 billion of investors' assets. At a later time this same eagerness to wheel and deal led two Bear Stearns High-Grade Structured Credit Strategies hedge funds, the Master Fund and the Enhanced Leverage Master Fund, into bankruptcy. I'm convinced this sandbox, in which millionaires play, is a disaster waiting for an opportunity to happen.

This gets us to the nub of it all. Your possession of substantial net worth will not guarantee you favorable investment results. Those individuals and organizations controlling the markets will continue to work in *their* best interests, not *yours*. It's your personal involvement and analysis of each opportunity which makes the difference. Always remember, your most reliable investment advisor will be the face in your mirror. You don't want to invest like a recognizable millionaire; you're better off if simply unnoticed.

22

PEDDLING GOLD: FLIMFLAM AT ITS FINEST

"Anything fo' half price is a bargain,
irregardless o' what ya' pay fo' it."
Mammy Yokum

The precious metals market, particularly gold and silver, is nothing less than dynamic. Whether it's suitable for profitable investment is another matter. The hour-long radio infomercial I recently tuned to proved too persuasive to ignore. I couldn't resist placing a telephone call to request a brochure guaranteed to provide "invaluable information available nowhere else."

Requesting the brochure took a bit of doing. Getting an assurance it would be sent required I first fend off three different "specialists," each encouraging "my immediate participation" by placing an order for gold or silver with their firm. Luckily I displayed as much perseverance as they; the last of them finally gave up and agreed to ship it off in the mail.

The brochure arrived a few days later. From it I gleaned not a word of objective information, but I most certainly viewed a work of art. The impressive cover is adorned with an enticing assortment of golden ingots. The presentation includes an informative 2,500-year history of gold, several graphs depicting the rise in the metal's value over the past dozen years, and comparisons between gold and alternative investments, particularly corporate securities and currency. Its implementation as a hedge against inflation is stressed repeatedly.

The brochure does not contain a hint ownership of gold can be anything but advantageous. Statements declaring gold ". . . means safety in any language," as well as ". . . provides protection against currency devaluations and continued market instability stemming from the global financial crisis," are dominant themes. If a single quotation must be chosen to summarize the impressively packaged 12-page offering, it is: "Gold is an internationally recognized asset with strong intrinsic value that stably increases in spite of fluctuating stock markets and temperamental economic environments."

So much for this particular purveyor and the impressions promoted. There are many other precious metals dealers advertising regularly in the media, and I suspect each delivers a similar pitch: *Buy gold now! It can only go up--up--and up!* And why shouldn't this be the message? It's unreasonable to expect a rational analysis of gold as an investment from a firm which makes its profit marketing the metal. Perhaps this may seem cynical, but it's claimed, and rightly so, by necessity all marketing schemes must be cynically devised. Now let me provide my view of gold as an investment. Regardless of whether I've accurately analyzed the variables, at least you may be sure, with no conflicting interests at stake, I'll exhibit no bias. But first, let's flash back in time to get an historical perspective of the metal's performance.

An appropriate date to start our viewing is 1833—exactly one century before the world found itself in the depths of perhaps the severest and most prolonged depression in mankind's recent history. And during this one-hundred-year-period the world price of gold remained nearly unchanged at between $19 and $25 per ounce. Not until the early 1930's, when the price of the metal became regulated by government fiat, did its value began to fluctuate. By 1934 the value of gold settled in at $35 per ounce, largely the result of the U. S. government, under newly-elected President Franklin D. Roosevelt, setting that as an established price together with a prohibition of gold ownership by its citizens. And there, at $35 per ounce, the price remained until 1970 when President Richard Nixon rescinded the policy, deregulating the metal, and once again permitted ownership by U. S. citizens. During the roughly four decades since its deregulation, the price of gold reacted to various market forces, often unpredictable. By 1980 its price exceeded $600 per ounce; by 1990 it could be purchased for $375; ten years later, in 2000, it dropped to $275; by 2005 it recovered to $450 and on August 22, 2011, a scant six years later, reached a record high of $1,908. Over the past year or so, its value fluctuated in the $1,200s. For whatever reason, gold has languished these past couple of years.

Enough of history—on to the future! What are the near-term predictions for the price of gold? We may ignore values bandied about by dealers. Their visions of the metal at $3,000 per ounce—or $4,000—or $5,000—indicate nothing more than an attempt to attract buyers. We shall, instead, consider the more reputable sources. Analysts surveyed by Bloomberg late last year forecasted a price per troy ounce of $1,925 by the fourth quarter of 2013. The bullion bank ScottiaMocatta envisioned a rise to $2,200, whereas the French Bank BNP Paribas predicted $1,825. On a less positive note, which proved to be the most accurate, Thomson Reuters GFMS anticipated a continual decrease during 2013. It's clear the diversity of predictions for 2013 and following years reflects the uncertainties of the global market. Simply stated, it's anyone's guess where both the economy and gold are headed.

Having declared it's anyone's guess where gold is headed, I'm now prepared to offer my opinion on exactly this. Let me preface my prediction by saying I believe three principal factors determine gold prices over the foreseeable future, and for our purposes I consider *foreseeable* as extending only through this decade. What may happen in the years beyond 2020 becomes increasingly less related to anything we can anticipate or control. These three factors are (1) inflation in the economy (2) governmental intervention (3) intrinsic use of gold. Let's look at each of these.

(1) Inflation in the Economy. A conventional belief exists, perhaps accurately, that rapid inflation in an economy will cause gold prices to rise. In characterizing inflation, we'll accept the definition of *The American Heritage Dictionary of the English Language, Fourth Edition*, 2000, which states:

> A persistent increase in the level of consumer prices or a persistent decline in the purchasing power of money, caused by an increase in available currency and credit beyond the proportion of available goods and services.

If we look no further than the uncontrolled spending and increasing national debt our nation's leaders promote, we cannot help but conclude a high rate of inflation will follow. If our presumption is correct, this will spur a rise in gold prices. Chalk up one vote for an increase.

(2) Governmental Intervention. Whether or not uncontrolled inflation will result from our nation's spending policies, there can be no doubt our economy is nowhere near recovered from the miseries of these past half-dozen years. My belief is we're in a depression, not a recession, with high unemployment continuing as a major drag on the economy as our citizens' suffering persists. Regardless of your political experience or economic expertise, there is really no way you can predict what action a government may take as an economy continues to unravel. As an example, look at how the tiny island nation of Cyprus in March of 2013 recently attempted to bail itself out of financial problems: by stealing its citizens' bank deposits. Regardless of the country, elected officials generally specialize in getting elected to public office, rather than in effectively resolving problems after being elected. We may only guess as to what precious metals regulations our government may enact. I'm afraid this second factor cannot guide us in predicting the direction gold prices will take.

(3) Intrinsic Use of Gold. We are now at what I believe to be the crux in determining future gold prices. Central to my reasoning is a fundamental reality: Except for its use in ornamentation, the metal possesses no commercially viable application. It can be admiringly gazed at, sensually fondled, and tastelessly drooled upon, but that's where its use ends. Simply stated, the value of gold is what a buyer can be induced to pay for it. I contend the fundamental value of any investment relates to the income flow it produces. And an investor in gold who sees

its value plummet can resort to no money-generating application while waiting to see if the market corrects itself. This lack of income generation does not portend well for gold. Cast one ballot in the downward direction.

I'll now summarize my expectations as to where I see gold heading over the next eight to ten years. Fundamental to my prognosis is the recognition the rapid escalation in price per ounce over the past half-dozen years is contrary to its historical trend. I acknowledge, of course, vast fortunes may be made through involvement in precious metals, and at times it can seem almost magical. However, when it comes to our personal investment program, we must put fantasy aside. The gold frenzy is quite recent; it's my experience what rises rapidly normally declines the same way.

I'll now insert another factor into the mix. I'm convinced the escalation in gold prices in recent years is attributable to a combination of two realities: First, that most investors have been deprived of any viable investments. Money market funds and CDs pay next to nothing; bonds appear hazardous if interest rates rise as many predict; and dividend yields remain at an historic low. Real estate is finally beginning to show promise, though its recovery is measured by the prevalence of short sales and the percentage of homes still underwater. Sophisticated real estate investment is unavailable for most persons. So, with no truly enticing investments to attract the public, gold is offered as an acceptable alternative.

The second half of the reality is evident to anyone paying attention. For the past few years precious metals, and particularly gold, continues to be touted from every conceivable forum. Talk show hosts pitch it; television ads praise it; financial advisors of every stripe are hired to recommend it; full-hour infomercials extol it. You cannot spend fifteen minutes in any media environment without being told gold is the investment of the century and its value will rise forever. As expected, there are legions of poor innocents who, burned by securities or real estate, are eager to travel the one sure road to everlasting wealth. Thus gold is effectively peddled, and as long as brisk sales continue, its price will resist a warranted collapse. It's my belief, however, at some point this market will return to earth.

I'll conclude with a final thought. Whether or not gold ascends further into the stratosphere is not nearly as meaningful as the question: Is gold a wise investment? My response must be negative. Despite recommendations to the contrary, there's no sound justification for investment in precious metals, whether as the base metal, the specie, or stock in related companies. The markets for gold, silver, and the like long ago entered the pseudo-religious realm, with adherents extolling their virtues, much as with Scientology or transcendental meditation. These markets are, by their nature, subject to manipulation, so performance cannot rationally be predicted.

23

JUSTICE DENIED

Justice is blind!
Aye, blind she is . . .
and deaf . . .
and dumb . . .
and got a wooden leg!

Over the past years I've developed some strong attitudes concerning the evolution of the justice system in this country. Those of you who regularly follow my financial column may question why my personal bias on this subject finds its way into an article customarily devoted to the subject of money. It's a fair complaint, so read on and decide for yourself whether the two subjects are perhaps more related than you might have first imagined.

Here in this second decade of the twenty-first century, the United States conducts a unique criminal justice system. Thanks to the "War on Drugs," prison cells are filled with non-violent drug users. At the same time large numbers of violent felons avoid incarceration after their offenses are negotiated down to lesser offenses—this, as prisons throughout the nation operate in excess of one hundred percent capacity. Even those sentenced to death for heinous murders remain on hold, often for more than a quarter century, while the court system processes countless appeals. And all the while our country's leaders vow to make criminal justice "fair" while we "get tough on crime."

Does any of this make sense? I'm afraid so, though in a perverse way. Never ignore the fact crime is big business, and not just as Al Capone might have understood. To the people who make criminal justice their occupation, fighting crime means spending money. The constant refrain from this group is that only by a constant infusion of money can lawlessness be combated. And the group is huge—lawyers, court employees, police, prison guards, contractors that build prisons, alarm system companies, the parole system, psychologists and psychiatrists, drug treatment hospitals—the list is endless.

As a matter of comparison, be aware over a century ago a small mid-western community experienced a rat infestation. The local town Council, in its wisdom, enacted a rat-removal ordinance offering to pay 25 cents for each rat-tail delivered to the city office. As expected, within a short time many people operated rat farms with the tails harvested for profit. And this is precisely what our criminal justice system now is—a giant rat-tail farm.

Only a country as wealthy as ours can support such a system. A poorer nation must handle crime as reality requires: summary courts, abbreviated appeals, minimally equipped and staffed prisons, and an inmate population to pay for its keep by actual "hard labor"—in short, criminals dealt with as the undesirable nuisance to society they are.

We, on the other hand, maintain a labyrinth in which the criminal constitutes a valuable asset, and where the meting out of justice and protection of the citizen ceases to be a primary goal. The law-breaker is peripheral to all this, of course, as influential political and economic groups vie for the benefits. In my view, the system operates primarily to distribute spoils, with little concern for its effect on crime. Under these circumstances it's clear why law enforcement agencies and legislative bodies assume the stances they do. As no real action can be taken to address problems—let alone resolve them—public officials simply placate the public by faking it. Embarrassed by crime, legislatures regularly increase the severity of punishment. At the same time, disturbed by the administration of the process, appellate courts seek to reinforce civil rights by tightening evidentiary rules. We are clearly making the worst of both worlds.

One other part of the problem is, as a society we are undecided as to who the prisons shall house, and for what purpose. This institutionalized schizophrenia is nowhere near resolution and contributes to a massive increase in inmate population. Of even greater significance is the polarizing effect on the law-enforcement community. Only a courageous governor will dare resist the influence of a powerful prison-guard union. The ability of such groups to lobby aggressively is something with which every aspiring office-seeker must reckon. It's no longer a matter of the tail wagging the dog—in reality the dog and the tail have changed places. It's painfully clear prisons now exist more to provide employment and benefits than to house criminals.

How shall things be resolved? In all likelihood there will be no resolution until the criminal problem in America ceases to be viewed from the customary standpoint of punishment, deterrence, rehabilitation, and warehousing—all approaches that require additional money. Only when we as a society begin to make *elimination of criminality* the primary goal will there be a pragmatic approach to the problem. Exactly what this means in practical terms is open to dispute. There's the risk, of course, of creating the sort of structure which operated during the waning years in the Soviet Union. At that time novelist and historian Aleksandr Solzhenitsyn described Soviet justice as a garbage disposal system judged exclusively by its efficiency. However without embracing at least a portion of this concept, all we will see is a continuation of business as usual.

In the final analysis, we as a civilized community must learn to distinguish between persons involved in self-destructive activities we will tolerate, and felons to be dealt with harshly. Once we make this distinction, the latter should then be treated as suggested by the eighteenth century King of Prussia, Frederick II: "For infamous fellows we shall want infamous punishments."

24

THE WORLD
OF THE IPO

The real beneficiaries of most systems
are those who administer the system.

On Friday, May 18, 2012, the long-awaited Initial Public Offering (IPO) of Facebook, a most popular social-networking enterprise, became reality. Throughout the day an eager investing public subscribed to some 500 million shares of its common stock at prices which ranged between $38 and $45 per share. Although the offering was vigorously touted and enthusiastically embraced for many days before its offering, not a great deal of thought appears to have been devoted to the company's actual value. Its reported earnings during 2011 revealed the opening price of $38 to be at a Price Earnings (P/E) Ratio in excess of 100, perhaps eight times higher than a prudent investor might be justified in paying. The rationalization for such a high P/E Ratio centered upon Facebook's 900 million accounts, which somehow suggested limitless growth and eventual profitability.

Before I comment on the bizarre aftermath of what deserved to go down in stock market history as "Black Friday," you deserve a glimpse into the world of the IPO. A word of caution: Unless you're a principal in a firm offering newly created stock to the public through an initial public offering, avoid acquisition of stock in this way, despite the source of the recommendation. Consider the typical scenario. The private corporation, whose two-year financial history reveals $10 million in accumulated losses, goes public for the first time. Five million shares are authorized, with an opening share price set at $12. On the day of the offering the complement is fully subscribed, at prices ranging from $25 to $45, closing the day at $35. Do not expect as an outsider there is a bonanza reserved for you. The profits will be distributed among the favored few: the principals, accountants, attorneys, and other professionals who assemble the package, and the one or more investment houses which market the shares. On the following day the outside purchaser awakens to learn of five hundred shares acquired at $35 each. Ninety days later it becomes clear the corporation is devoid of both assets and prospects, with its shares quoted at 13½ bid. In the spirit of the foundering private company, the IPO subscribes to the time-honored tradition: *Don't go broke . . . go public!*

If in the immediate aftermath of the Facebook IPO the newly issued shares simply meandered on to their eventual trading range—whether up, down or sideways, as is common with such issuances—nothing deserves comment. However, in less than twenty-four hours the first wrinkle appeared as controversy arose over allegations of misconduct by one of the prime marketers of the issue, Morgan Stanley, a global financial firm headquartered in New York with more than 1,300 offices and 60,000 employees, which services a diversified group of corporations, governments and financial institutions. The cause of the outrage: As the shares of the public offering began to trade, officials of Morgan Stanley were reported to have secretly informed their large, well-heeled, long-time clients of a reevaluation *downward* of Facebook's anticipated earnings while continuing to market shares to the rabble with no such warning. How such a revelation became known is as yet uncertain; possibly some disgruntled insider blew the whistle.

The Morgan Stanley revelation caused an immediate upheaval throughout the market. Within seventy-two hours of the IPO, Facebook share value, which had ended the first day at $38.23, fell in open trading by more than 13% to $33 per share. As expected, the churning continued, with the per share value down to $26.95 and two class action lawsuits filed, all within two weeks following the IPO. As expected, numerous legislators proclaimed the need for more oversight of the securities industry. Actually there's justification for such scrutiny, if not for the fact such laws are routinely enacted in the aftermath of all such controversies and invariably amount to nothing. In the class actions, only the litigating attorneys profit; whatever meaningful fines and penalties the SEC extracts will be retained by them, not the victims; any legislation enacted will prove, as usual, to be ineffective.

If there's a fundamental underlying principal to be revealed in this recent Facebook fiasco, it's that the atrocities depicted are not unique to IPOs, but rather permeate all phases of the corporate world. The simple fact is the favoring of well-paying large clients to the detriment of smaller ones is a staple of the securities industry. In this regard, I'll share with you my vague recollections of an event occurring more than thirty years ago. It relates to one of America's then-major airlines, Braniff International

Airways, a firm operating from 1930 until 1982, primarily in the midwestern and southwestern United States as well as numerous foreign countries. Although highly profitable in its early years, the effects of the Airline Deregulation Act of 1978 adversely affected its operations. By early 1982 serious financial problems appeared obvious, at least to those on the inside.

What then transpired is still somewhat uncertain, as the testimony presented during the subsequent legal proceedings remains contradictory. However, a part of the story appears clear. Braniff hired the major multinational stock brokerage firm at the time, Merrill Lynch, controlling over $1.8 trillion in client assets, with offices in more than 40 countries around the world, to dispose of the company's common stock. With the full knowledge of all parties involved of a likely bankruptcy filing, Merrill Lynch began systematically marketing Braniff shares held by both holders of their major accounts, as well as Braniff's executives, to their multitude of customers of modest means. Over a period of some weeks the airline's stock was vigorously touted as sound, while the preferred clients unloaded hundreds of thousands of shares. And as planned from the onset, on May 11, 1982, the airline's CEO, Howard Putnam, left a courtroom at the Federal Courthouse in Brooklyn, New York, after failing to gain an extension from the airline's principal creditors. The following day, May 12th, Braniff Airways ceased all operation, ending 54 years of service.

There's an amusing postscript to relate which adds a second dimension to this tale. The investigation and litigation dragged on for two years afterward, but resulted in no particularly satisfactory conclusion for the victims. The money they lost never reappeared. The usual charges and recriminations bandied about in such cases continued to reverberate for awhile, but nothing of consequence resulted. Nonetheless, it can be said Merrill Lynch did not exactly escape unscathed. Though they never admitted guilt of any sort, the SEC taught them a lesson. As a token hand-slap, the SEC attached a padlock to the front door of Merrill's main New York City office for 30 days. Whether or not the back door remained accessible to clients and customers during that period was never disclosed.

If there is any moral to be drawn from the current Facebook episode, or the ancient Merrill Lynch/Braniff Airways saga, it's that every participant in the securities market must understand how the system works. Never ignore the fact that the practice known as "insider trading"—the buying and selling of a security on the basis of information unavailable to the general public—is routinely engaged in at every level. Although piously criticized and denied by all participants, and clearly a violation of the law, it can be declared to be a bedrock of the industry. It's my belief the ability of corporate insiders to manipulate all aspects of their companies, and profit from such transactions, is the principal reason the nation's public corporations exist.

25

CHASING FORECLOSURES: AN EXERCISE IN FORTITUDE

There is no calamity, however earth-shattering,
that does not offer the opportunity for some
persons to thrive on the misfortunes of others.

A newspaper advertisement, featuring a national celebrity enthusiastically promoting a real estate seminar, recently caught my attention. The pitch was one I'd seen before: Attendance at the weekend "Wealth Creating Conference," costing a mere $2,495, will enable the attendee to "...hit it big in the lucrative foreclosure market," and become "financially independent before the year is out." As my mind drifts back to past recollections, I envision the events which will transpire as each enthusiastic entrepreneur-to-be, having completed sixteen hours of instruction, attempts to put the information to profitable use. Ah, the picture comes through so clearly . . .

Ralph Adams is diligently applying the knowledge acquired at the foreclosure seminar he attended a month ago. As the instructor said, there's a fortune to be made picking up troubled properties. Why, it's simply a matter of application and diligence, and just one acquisition alone will more than pay back the $2,495 seminar cost. Yes, that's what the instructor said. It all seemed pretty clear at the time, and the foreclosure sale at which Ralph acquired a property at ten o'clock this morning couldn't have been less demanding, with his the only bid. To be a bit more accurate, in some western states it's a *trustee's sale*, the distinction being the proceeding is conducted outside the judicial system as opposed to a judicial foreclosure administered through the courts. Although there are meaningful differences, the terms are used interchangeably.

It's now six hours later, and after thirty-five fruitless minutes on telephone hold waiting to be informed of the amount due on a supplemental tax bill, he hangs up in disgust. This seems a matter not covered during the lectures, he recalls. Neither did the course clearly explain whether, after bidding in the property on a mortgage default, the senior lender might exercise its alienation clause and call the note due and payable. Perhaps the presentation should have devoted less time to testimonials and more to details. While pondering his next move, the phone rings. The voice at the other end identifies herself as a member of the law firm representing the former owner— and still occupant—of the acquired property. The message conveyed is clear and to the point: The notice to vacate delivered earlier in the day is defective and her client will vigorously resist any eviction action.

Ralph's education is just beginning. Though he doesn't yet realize it, he is in an arena replete with peril. The hardy souls that regularly participate in the foreclosure sale market quickly develop a set of cut and dried processes to minimize the inherent risks. Let me discuss briefly the four basic areas of uncertainty to be factored into this enterprise.

• **Shenanigans leading up to the foreclosure sale.** This can be a time of game-playing by all parties. The noteholder's financial stability can affect the progress of the foreclosure sale, particularly in the final stages, with repeated postponements of sale date not uncommon. The mortgagor (debtor) may attempt to delay matters through refinancing activity, sale escrow openings, bankruptcy filing, or side agreements with the holder. Again, postponements can result. All these activities can make the procedure a spastic event with a succession of sale dates which seem never to end.

• **Unanticipated clouds on the title.** Before an informed bid can be made, the bidder must know what obligations will remain on title after the foreclosure sale. All delinquent real estate taxes, senior mortgages, and unpaid association fees can be expected to remain against the property. In addition, although liens and encumbrances junior to the foreclosing beneficiary are normally wiped out, there can be exceptions. Certain items, notably mechanic's and IRS liens enjoy priority status. And finally, there are circumstances where various types of actions, particularly involving such matters as Medicaid fraud and child support claims, can contaminate a title long after acquisition. Although title insurance provides protection in the case of a normal purchase, such guarantees are far less comprehensive in a foreclosure sale.

• **Possession of the property.** Difficulties may be encountered in attempting to oust the prior owner or tenant in possession after acquiring ownership. It's unrealistic to expect cooperation from the dweller. My practice is to institute eviction action within hours after the sale. As any occupant becomes what is known as a *tenant at severance* upon transfer of title, the filing of an unlawful detainer action may often be commenced without even the need for service of a notice to quit. However, in the past few years, since commencement of "The Great Recession," the federal government has inserted itself into the mix, so a tenant enjoys special possession rights upon a foreclosure. I'll not get into the details here; you may research that on your own. Unfortunately, an inherent advantage is maintained by whoever holds possession, and the courts control the process. There are jurisdictions decidedly hostile to property owners as opposed to parties in possession. This can result in an extended waiting period between a submission for a default judgment (one in which the defendant fails to file a response) and the actual granting of the judgment wherein a writ of possession is issued. There are jurisdictions where four months is not uncommon. And while we're on the subject of delay, untold mischief is possible if the occupant files an action in bankruptcy. This automatically halts any eviction action proceeding in state court, transferring the matter to the federal bankruptcy court. It's not unusual for three months to elapse before the initial bankruptcy hearing.

• **Physical condition of the property**. It is rarely an easy matter to inspect the property prior to the foreclosure sale. The party in possession is often hostile and, as the Trustee conducting the sale can provide no help, the prospective bidder seldom views an interior. Furthermore, it's common when possession of the property is finally delivered, its condition can be abominable. I recall one house I acquired where, before departing, the prior owner smashed all double-pane windows, removed the light fixtures, carted off the front and garage doors, and destroyed all bathroom and kitchen appliances and cabinetry.

And so, for you entrepreneurs who plan to chase foreclosures, let me leave you with a few guidelines. Collect the information as best you can, recognizing you'll not get it all. Realize the more cash you have on hand after acquisition, the sounder will be your position. Most importantly, hedge your bet by limiting your bid so cash investment plus all anticipated obligations will not exceed a predetermined amount—my personal rule of thumb is 60 percent of the property's market value. And finally, hope for the best . . . but be prepared for the worst.

26

COLLEGE YOU
CAN AFFORD

Educational Doctrine of the Faith:
Academic excellence results from the
spending of money.

When it comes to budget-breaking for the average family, nothing compares with the costs of schooling. With high school for you or your offspring soon visible through the rear view mirror, college must be considered. To prosper in this society, higher education is necessary, and education must be selective as well as extensive. The trick is figuring out what to study—and where.

What to study requires a certain degree of clairvoyance. Who might have predicted in 1970, for example, many of the prestigious and sought-after masters in business administration degrees would, within a short ten years, have slight acceptance and negligible value? As universities throughout the nation hurriedly set up MBA courses to cash in on the fad, a skeptical analysis would have revealed many of the programs to be devoid of substance. What initially escaped the academic world became painfully obvious to the business community: many holders acquired an advanced degree of no consequence. Although this diploma, thanks to the internet age, regained some luster as a money-making accessory, its actual educational value is questionable. If there's a moral, it's the academic establishment cannot be relied upon to develop and implement meaningful courses of study. You, as the prospective student, must conduct your own investigation and make that determination for yourself.

When it comes to determining *where* to study, the options become even more confusing. If you believe the brochures of the major universities, you will conclude a graduate of other than a renowned institution is forever doomed to mediocrity. The official line is only *name* universities offer quality education. In this regard it's worth comparing the 2-year colleges with the 4-year schools as to value and educational opportunity.

From the standpoint of tuition, the standard community college normally is far less expensive, at least for legal residents of the district. Note, however, many jurisdictions impose a hefty surcharge for out-of-district students, which can dissipate any cost advantage. As to whether the lower cost is reflective of lower quality, there's disagreement. According to a past president of the University of California, the network of community colleges throughout that most populous state is little better than its high schools, and does not begin to compare in academic quality with the University system. Unquestionably his opinion would be echoed by the twenty-four members of the UC Board of Regents as well as most of the faculty members of the nine campuses. Though it's hard to refute such an authoritative group, a personal testimonial is in order. It was my good fortune to attend not one, but three, community colleges in Orange County during the years 1979-1981, completing courses in basic inorganic and organic chemistry. My next several years were spent at the University of California

Irvine completing the requirements for both a bachelor's and a master's degree in that subject. From this experience, I can say, without reservation, and contrary to the claims of our unnamed past president, the quality of instruction at the community college is superior in virtually every respect to that at the university. This is not to suggest there are no good instructors in the nation's universities. There *are!* Nor should you think all community college instructors are first rate. They *are not!* It's simply the quality of schooling seems generally to decline as the prestige of the institution increases. If there's a reason, it's because the 2-year schools exist to provide education, whereas the universities, particularly those offering various graduate degrees, derive their sustenance in a different manner. For a well-documented view of the role of the modern university in America, you should read *ProfScam,* a 1988 in-depth analysis by Charles J. Sykes.

Whether or not you commence your higher education at a 2-year institution, the bachelor's and higher degrees must be earned at the more expensive university. Where you choose will be a personal decision, and there is no end to the recommendations you'll receive. Numerous guides are found in the college reference sections of most bookstores which evaluate the many schools, and you may be inclined to browse through them. Probably the most comprehensive is the recent (2013) edition of *Barron's Profiles of American Colleges,* retailing at Amazon for $20.90, and includes an attached CD. Its superbly-indexed pages are overwhelmingly thorough, and include information on housing, programs of study, faculty, classrooms, student life and financial aid, as well as much else on 1,650 institutions. Although the data to be found there may be of some peripheral value, my personal belief is there's not much useful academic guidance to be gleaned, particularly as to assessing the quality of education offered. The reason for this is the learning a student will absorb in any venue has nothing much to do with the many features described and evaluated by the college guides. Most of the information presented is puffery.

I subscribe to the principle of *college-on-the-cheap*. The first two years of post-secondary education, the freshman and sophomore years, are pursued at a local community college. Here in my state of California, tuition costs are $46 per semester-unit. With a little counselor guidance, subjects which are fully transferable toward a university degree can be chosen. In this way, a year's course of study, consisting of a full load of 30 units, is available at a $1,380 tuition charge.

The next two years, as a Junior and Senior, will be earned at a state university. Tuition charges vary with each state, but legal residents generally enjoy low preferential rates. The annual tuition for a full academic load at the California State University system, not living on campus, is currently $6,188 plus about $2,000 for books, supplies and miscellaneous fees.

My next dictum is the student live at and commute from home during the full course of study. This requires cooperative parents, of course, and perhaps some negotiation will be in order between all parties involved. Family dynamics change as children grow into adults, but the favorable result of an economically obtained degree for the progeny should encourage compromises.

For those of you unfamiliar with modern schooling, the price of textbooks is now something awesome. It's not unusual for hundreds of dollars to be spent on them each semester. It's for this reason I recommend used books.

Unfortunately, most university bookstores which deal in them set prices approaching those of a new issue. Your best bet will often be purchasing them directly from a student just completing the course, provided, of course, the textbook is not continually revised so to prevent its being resold and used again. But in any event, there's a serendipitous benefit to a used book. It's not unusual to find helpful underlining of important sections as well as worthwhile comments written in the margins.

My final recommendation is the student spends each summer between academic years working at a paying job. The one benefit is obvious: money earned will help finance the forthcoming school year. But there's an additional value. There is a component in toil that instills appreciation for what learning is all about. The mixture of education and experience is a winning combination.

I'm thoroughly convinced two years at a local community college followed by the junior and senior years at a reasonably priced state university is the way to go. This is because scholastic benefit depends more upon the student's efforts than anything else. Neither the architectural characteristics of the campus and classrooms nor the credentials of the professors will determine the extent of learning acquired by a motivated student. My mastery of algebra is in no way diminished because my classroom was a primitively lighted and ventilated Quonset hut at Los Angeles City College. Similarly my grasp of partnership law did not suffer owing to a nameless and faceless course instructor located in a post office box at the LaSalle Institute correspondence school some two thousand miles away. Admittedly a smiling and enthusiastic professor in a prestigious university will add a touch of stature to the process, but the student who strives to learn will do so regardless of the accouterments.

Let me share my personal bias with you. Unless you or your parents have more money than you know what to do with, attendance at an acclaimed university represents an unwarranted expense. The time will come when your textbooks have been sold, your course notes burned, the names of your instructors forgotten, and your framed diploma relegated to a wall at which you rarely glance. At that point your education is what is left in your head. This is what really counts.

And here's a thought for those critics who contend a degree from an institution without an exalted reputation will forever stigmatize its holder. To you, I pose this question: Do you actually know from what schools your dentist, attorney, accountant, and physician received their bachelors' degrees?

As my final word on higher education, you're invited to ponder the following lines of verse.

◆　　◆　　◆

EDUCATION FOR THE MASSES

There was a Ruler, bright and bold,
In ancient times, as it is told,
Before the academic mold
　　To which we've grown committed.
He felt that learning was amiss,
And yearned for the antithesis,
That the untutored populace
　　Could yet be benefited.

Though his ken topped the apogee,
It grieved him very much to see,
That others had, compared to he,
   An education shoddy.
And as he had it in his might,
Authority to set things right,
He thus bestowed, to his delight,
   Degrees on everybody.

The land was suddenly awash,
In literate and highbrow bosh.
Displays of knowledge, crassly swash,
   Good judgment in remission.
While idiotic concepts soared
From sage advisors by the horde,
Professors, all — with mortarboard,
   A most grotesque condition.

Philosophers, at every turn,
Spewed concepts that none could discern,
With understanding far astern,
   And logic nonexistent.
On every corner scholars preened,
Each one *cum laude*, so it seemed,
All thoughts were equally esteemed,
   Thought often inconsistent.

That Ruler, though to all endeared,
Caused learning to be commandeered.
And when *all* judgment is revered,
   We cease to be demanding.
Thus surely when the time arrives,
That mock equality applies,
No one will *dare* to criticize,
   A third-rate understanding.

And so you clearly get the view,
When every college pushes through
Each simpleton that asks it to,
   True worth must be diminished.
Of one thing it's a certainty,
And really, it's not hard to see,
When everyone's a PhD,
   Then education's finished.

27

ROTH IRA CONVERSIONS: IT'S IN THE NUMBERS

Don't make decisions on emotion or conjecture.
Important matters must be thought through.

Over the years I've compared the relative benefits of traditional IRAs with those of Roth IRAs. Despite an inability to deduct contributions, I invariably advocate Roth for most qualifying persons. This is due to its fully tax-free treatment as opposed to the merely tax-deferred character of a traditional. This benefit can even make it advantageous to convert a traditional into a Roth, and on occasions I've advocated this maneuver. However, doing so must not be done without weighing the consequences, and this means number crunching. Let's take a closer look at the possibilities. Please stick with me as I crunch the numbers.

Consider a 30-year-old unmarried resident of Florida with annual taxable income of $50,000 and a traditional IRA valued at $100,000. If we presume those assets, skillfully managed, compound at 7½% per annum (not unreasonable over a third-of-a-century), they'll grow tax-deferred over 35 years until retirement to become $1.25 million. By contrast, we might roll the assets into a Roth IRA that will grow to a like sum over the years, though doing so triggers its being taxed initially as ordinary income which, superimposed on the other earnings, calculates to a tax payment of $27,350. If paid with money from outside the account so to avoid penalties, it means liquidating personal assets. Had those funds not been so dissipated, they would have compounded over 35 years at an after-tax rate of about 5½% to become $178,000.

At this point we'll compare the two retirement cash flows: income on $1,250,000 from the Roth IRA or that from $1,428,000—$1.25 million in the traditional IRA plus $178,000 personal assets. Presuming each can generate 7½%, the respective annual cash flows are $93,750 tax-free versus $107,100 taxable. Although the comparative advantage of tax-free versus taxable income 35 years into the future is not easily predicted, it's unlikely the citizens' burden will by then have eased. It's plausible to expect, in the great bountiful society of the future, six-figure income will be taxed at no less than 25%. If so, the annual net cash-in-pocket upon retirement will be $93,750 from the Roth rollover as against $80,325 by abstaining. It's quite clear the Roth rollover is a benefit in this case.

We'll now modify our example just a little: Our Florida resident becomes a Californian, and in doing so consumes all disposable cash outside the IRA account. Over 35 years the traditional IRA will experience no change; it will still grow to $1.25 million. But conversion becomes more expensive for two reasons: a 9.3% state income tax as opposed to no tax in Florida, and penalties for withdrawal of IRA funds to pay these taxes—10% to the federal government plus 2.5% to California for any amount liquidated. The governments thus receive jointly

$41,885 ($36,650 taxes and $5,235 penalties), resulting in a Roth IRA balance starting at $58,115. At 7½% annually over 35 years, it grows to $730,400. Our comparative retirement cash flows now become $43,590 tax-free from the Roth versus $93,750 taxable from the traditional. It's clear, unless tax rates ultimately become near-confiscatory, the Roth rollover does not pay for itself.

You now possess a blueprint by which to analyze whether or not conversion from a traditional to a Roth IRA makes economic sense. Variables that affect your calculations will be the amount of IRA assets converted, individual's age upon conversion, anticipated age at retirement, state tax and penalty rates, and source of funds from which the conversion tax will be paid. In general, prospects for conversion are most promising with a lesser amount of assets, greater time span between conversion and retirement, low state income tax rate, and sufficient available cash to avoid dipping into IRA assets for the tax payment. As a rule of thumb, conversions seem to make sense for persons under age 35, in states with low income tax rates—or better yet, *none*, such as Florida, Texas, Nevada, and a few others—and when the amount to be rolled is relatively small. However, under all circumstances, I strongly advocate you actually grind out your numbers before you commit.

Before we depart this subject, and while our brains are still in gear, there's a matter which warrants consideration. If you're one of the unlucky ones for whom rollover is not practicable, is there anything you might do to improve your situation, perhaps down the line? Let's look back to the example of our California resident who will retain the traditional IRA, possibly adding contributions to it over the years. At retirement, assets might well exceed $1.5 million and generate substantial retirement income—fully taxable, of course. When the day arrives that a California-generated salary is no longer needed, a question comes immediately to mind: If, following retirement, one moves from a state collecting income tax to one that does not, must taxes be paid to the state in which the contributions originated? Although some state tax collectors issue proclamations implying otherwise, it's my belief the answer is *no*. If the new state of residence is one with no income tax, IRA distributions will incur no state taxes regardless of where the IRA assets were amassed.

Regarding state IRA taxation, I'll insert a caution. If, as a long-time Californian, you claim Nevada residence by using a friend's address in Laughlin while continuing to occupy your home in Long Beach, you probably won't get away with it. If tax avoidance is sufficiently important, you'd better do it for real. This means you actually take up full-time residence in the new state, register to vote there, get your driver's license and auto plates there, take your mail there, and conduct your life as a citizen of the new state. If you try to arrange it by charade, you're likely to end up with the worst of both worlds: the inconvenience of an illusory change of address together with full taxation of your IRA distributions.

It will not be fair to conclude this analysis without a final warning. Everything I've said and every calculation I've performed is only valid if eventual distribution of assets from the Roth IRA remain tax-free. You should be aware Australia, not a nation with a reputation of stealing from its citizens, has its superannuation fund similar to our Roth IRA. This government recently announced new rules which penalize citizens who had set aside savings for their retirement. Any income over $100,000 drawn from a superannuation fund will now be taxed at 15%. Previously, all such income was tax-free. You must recognize if this can happen in Australia, which still has reasonable debt levels despite years of deficit spending, it can certainly happen in the United States.

28

HOW TO DISPOSE OF AN UNWANTED PARTNER

When Jesse James took your money, it was
called robbery. When Al Capone took your
money, it was called extortion. When Uncle Sam
takes your money, it's called taxation.

For those of us schooled in the history of early twentieth century America, personages like John Dillinger, Baby Face Nelson, and Machine Gun Kelly, are familiar names. But perhaps the most notorious of all was "Big Al" Capone, a vicious Chicago racketeer who perfected, among other atrocities, the protection racket. He employed a straight-forward method: He declared himself to be a partner of local shopkeepers, offering to protect them from misfortune for a fee. As expected, those refusing to make the payments encountered misfortune—courtesy of "Big Al."

Now that you understand how partnerships are created, you might consider how best to deal with *your* business partner. Did I hear you say you're an independent entrepreneur having no partner? Oh yes you do. It's your, and everybody's, favorite uncle . . . Sam. He participates in your prosperity. Whatever profits you earn, not a dime of it will you fail to share with him. That's the way it is with partners, you see.

I know what you're thinking. You'd prefer to do without this partner. Well, I understand your attitude, but it's not advisable to ignore him. He's here to stay. However, you might give some thought to shaving his percentage of the take. Let me explain. Over the past couple of decades the government developed an insatiable appetite for money. Of the tills they've tapped, none proved more lucrative than from the income flowing to the mass of working citizens. In particular, individuals earning more than about $30,000 per year from a business—truly a modest amount—must contribute a substantial portion to the Internal Revenue Service. A few figures will illustrate the dilemma. As a sole proprietor, your next dollar over the $30,000 will incur a 25% income tax plus a 15.3% FICA tax, for a total of 40.3%. And if you're fortunate(?) enough to live in California, as I do, you can add another 9.3% in state income tax.

As grim as it sounds, all is not hopeless. Some of you, generally the self-employed with a certain amount of investment or other non-earnings income, enjoy some flexibility. We shall now explore what avenue is open to those of you in this circumstance. The following scenario will give you an approach to the problem.

Consider the plight of Sally Sellmore, self-employed real estate broker and investor, age forty-five, unmarried, $60,000 net annual investment income from rents, mortgage interest, and dividends plus $40,000 net business income from real estate brokerage. Only the $40,000 of business income, reported on Form 1040 Schedule C, is subject to social security tax. At 15.3 percent this amounts to $6,120 per year. However, she can avoid this cost by simply forming a Type C corporation from which to operate the brokerage. As corporate income, it is FICA exempt.

Concurrently, another benefit is a more favorable income tax rate. Corporate income is taxed federally at 15 percent on the first $50,000, this far preferable to the 25 and 28 percent rates superimposed on $60,000 of other income. The tax reduction on her $40,000 of income is about 12 percent, for an additional saving of $4,800. Taking into account both FICA and federal income taxes, an annual $10,920 in reduction is possible. This is meaningful.

As simple as it sounds, there are other matters to consider. Foremost among them is the question: what becomes of the corporate income? If passed on as salary it becomes taxable mostly at 28 percent plus a FICA obligation of 7.65 percent each to corporation and Ms. Sellmore; there is no advantage in that. A second possibility is a periodic dividend distribution. Although this avoids the social security consideration, it raises the specter of double taxation: 15 percent to the corporation plus a second hit at her personal tax bracket rate. Once again there's no advantage.

How can the problem be resolved? For this technique to work, the income must remain in the corporation as undistributed earnings, meaning that it not be required for personal living expenses. With Ms. Sellmore's investment income, and reasonable frugality, she can pull it off. Thus the corporation will, over a period of years, accumulate net worth. This, however, raises an additional hurdle called the *accumulated earnings surtax* of 15 percent. The Internal Revenue Service does not like to see corporations hoard earnings as it interferes with the double taxation they understandably find to their liking. Fortunately there is some leeway. An accumulated earnings credit of $250,000 prevents assessment of the tax until the aggregation reaches that amount. Also, any portion of the cache used for reasonable needs of the business may be further excluded. With prudent management, "reasonable needs" can be found for these funds. What sort of purposes, you might ask? Here is where it gets stickier. To avoid *personal holding company* status, and yet another 15 percent surtax, the corporation must restrict its investments so not to exceed specific percentages of certain types of income, most importantly interest, dividends, rents, and royalties. As you see, though legitimate tax avoidance requires mastery of the details and a degree of discipline, it can be worth the effort. In this example over a ten-year period, by this single stratagem, $109,200 can be kept from the tax collector.

A final thought: Let me address the complaint I sense you're about to advance. You're concerned the method I've just described will deprive you of a vital element in your planned retirement: Social Security income. This is a subject I've considered in extensive depth and will summarize with a testimonial and a moral. Testimonial: When, in 1981, I determined social security to be an unsound investment, I effectively opted out of the system by the method outlined above. Because of this, my net worth today is substantially higher than if I continued to contribute. Moral: Social Security, as it functions today, is an exercise in robbing one group of citizens to favor another. For practical purposes, money taken from you in FICA payments is lost to you forever.

29

A CURE FOR ALZHEIMER'S DISEASE?

Funds for research and treatment of
garden variety senility are hard-come-by.
"Alzheimer's Disease" works much better.

Although the intent of the writings presented here is to counsel the reader on financial well-being, I can't resist sharing with you this article devoted to mental well-being. You cannot deny, being economically well-off isn't much fun if you don't have the mentality to enjoy it. What I offer here is a compilation of thoughts and speculations I came up with few years ago. Please read on.

On Wednesday, November 24, 2010, the American Medical Association published a study by the Pennington Biomedical Research Center of Baton Rouge, Louisiana, which found a combination of aerobic exercise and resistance training greatly benefits persons with type 2 diabetes. This is but one more bit of evidence demonstrating the healthful effects of physical activity, now recognized as beneficial for all sorts of ailments. Where this fits into the title subject, Alzheimer's disease, will be addressed shortly, but first we must take a closer look at the affliction.

For most of the 20th Century, the diagnosis of Alzheimer's disease, named for the German neuropathologist Alois Alzheimer who first described the condition in 1902, was relegated to individuals who displayed symptoms of senile dementia between the ages of 45 and 65. The terminology changed in 1977 following a conference of professionals in the field, who concluded the symptoms observed were much the same independent of age. Thereafter the term Alzheimer's disease became universally used.

Today the dominant Alzheimer's organization is the National Institute of Neurological Disorders and Stroke (NINDS), a division of the National Institutes of Health (NIH), established and funded by the U.S. government. NIH is divided into two parts: the "Extramural" parts are responsible for the funding of biomedical research outside of NIH, while the "Intramural" parts conduct research. It works toward that mission by conducting research in its own laboratories, supporting the research of non-Federal scientists (in universities, medical schools, hospitals, and research institutions throughout the country and abroad), helping in the training of research investigators, and fostering communication of medical and health sciences information. NINDS also funds clinical research related to diseases and disorders of the brain and nervous system. By necessity, NIH and NINDS are closely allied with the medical industry, and particularly the psychiatric community. As you can understand, with massive sums of money regularly distributed, intense political pressures and lobbying are at work in every aspect of operation.

This gets us to the subject at hand: Alzheimer's disease. Reports on the research, studies, and tests conducted on this malady are virtually limitless. However, the results of these reports can be concisely summarized:

1) Although the course of the disease is unique for each individual, there are many common symptoms.

2) The early stages of the condition are difficult to diagnose.

3) Numerous competing hypotheses exist trying to explain the cause of the disease.

4) Experimental vaccines have been tried, but none with any significant effect.

5) To date, the safety and efficacy of more than 400 pharmaceutical treatments have been investigated. None show particularly favorable results.

6) At present, there is no definitive evidence to support that any particular measure is effective in preventing the ailment.

7) There is no cure for Alzheimer's disease; available treatments offer relatively small symptomatic benefit but remain palliative in nature.

8) The cause and progression of the ailment are not well understood. Currently used treatments arguably offer a small symptomatic benefit; no treatments to delay or halt its progression are yet available . . . *with but one almost unnoticed sentence in a NINDS report: "Physical activity is associated with a reduced risk of AD."* Please take note:

A comprehensive analysis of this sentence will follow, but first I must broach a somewhat unrelated subject.

There is a well-known medical impairment known as *cerebral hypoxia*; it refers to a reduced supply of oxygen to the brain. Its effect on the body is impairment of brain function. One common cause is stroke, categorized by the severity and location of the brain's oxygen deprivation, the most serious and often fatal being total oxygen deprivation known as *cerebral anoxia*. Other abnormalities can also cause cerebral hypoxia or anoxia: severe asthma, various sorts of anemia, ascent from a deep water dive, flying at high altitudes in an un-pressurized cabin, and various traumatic events such as choking, drowning, strangulation, drug overdoses and shock. Brain damage can occur both during and after oxygen deprivation. During deprivation, cells die due to an increasing acidity in the brain tissue, and these cells are very sensitive to reduced oxygen levels. Once deprived of oxygen they will begin to die off within five minutes.

The physiological effects of oxygen deprivation are also well documented. When localized to a specific part of the brain, brain damage will be localized to that region. Damage to the left side typically causes problems with speech and language. Damage to the right side may interfere with the ability to express emotions or interpret what one sees.

The final observation on this subject of oxygen deprivation comes from an Internet blog I stumbled upon: *My Crohn's and Colitis Blog*. It included this inquiry by J. Burgess: "Can anyone tell me what the effects of long-term oxygen deprivation are, as in mild chronic untreated allergic asthma?" The response from another participant said: "Dear J. Burgess, I can't claim to be an expert on this, but my fiancée was a chronic and unstable asthmatic for many years. The effects I recognize as being directly linked to oxygen deficiency were: 1. Clubbing of fingers and toes   2. Confusion and mental 'fog'   3. Poor circulation, particularly to the extremities"

With the preceding information, documentary evidence, and a lone testimonial as my input, I'm now prepared to offer a theory as to one possible cause of Alzheimer's disease as well as pose a pair of hypothetical questions relating to its prevention.

First, the theory: It's abundantly clear many of the symptoms commonly associated with dementia of all sorts can be related to oxygen deprivation. Let's take a closer look at the normal aging process. As persons get older they become less physically active. Singles tennis played in the 20's is replaced by doubles in the 50's and finally by observing the grandchildren at play in the 70's. The 4-mile run performed three times weekly by a fit 36-year-old is no longer possible when, at 53, the knee joint fails. The aches and pains which come in the later years dissuade many from taking an exhilarating five mile round-trip hike to the post office. It's quicker and easier by auto.

Another factor changes as the years progress. With a reduction in physical activity is added a slowdown in metabolism, particularly the body's failure to burn fats that otherwise end up lining the artery walls. As the deposits accumulate, the blood vessels narrow and the flow of blood—and with it oxygen it carries to all parts of the body—is reduced.

We must now ask a pointed question: What is one notable result of this more sedentary lifestyle? It is less blood flows through the arteries—and in particular through the two carotid arteries which supply oxygen to the brain. As physical activity lessens, supply of oxygen to the brain must similarly lessen. In an otherwise healthy senior, is this reduction sufficient to bring on the effects of dementia? Perhaps it is; perhaps it is not.

This is now the time for the two hypothetical questions, designed to focus on a single aspect of Alzheimer's disease: prevention.

1. If the flow of blood to the brain, and with it the oxygen it carries, can be sustained, through regular cardiovascular exercise, into a person's senior years, might it result in an effective preventative to dementia?

2. Is it plausible, given a favorable answer to question 1, a sufficient number of persons in their 50's, 60's, 70's, and beyond can be induced to regularly engage in activities necessary to effect a positive result?

I might add, these questions are not hypothetical to me. Over the past fifty years I've regularly engaged in the sort of exercises that speed the heart rate. Although the running, tennis and bicycling I once engaged in pretty well ended years ago, I've maintained, now into my 80's, a daily schedule of an hour of continuous swimming and 30 minutes of weights. I don't know whether this is one of the major reasons nothing seriously afflicts me. Perhaps I'm just lucky. And as for dementia, I didn't need a ghostwriter to compose this article. I'll leave it to you to decide whether Alzheimer's has set in.

A final question, rhetorical I'm afraid, is in order. Why did NIH and its NINDS division never pose the questions I just asked? Is it because my theory is so outlandish as to be rejected out of hand? Though it may sound conspiratorial, I can think of another reason. For the many organizations which work closely with NINDS, there are fortunes to be garnered in studies conducted, research reports, testing and retesting, drug experimentation, and all the allied activity to be lobbied through Congress. On the other hand, there is not much profit to be reaped by encouraging oldsters to vigorously walk four miles at a clip or visit the local YMCA for a daily swim. In short, it's business as usual. Why would you expect anything different?

30

A THIMBLEFUL
OF PROSPERITY

Most persons don't accomplish the things they
want because they never get around to it.

Over the past several decades I've been an advocate
of prosperity. During this time I've encouraged people to
save and invest for their future. My financial newsletter, as
well as a regular flow of articles, stresses the importance of
amassing assets. In these writings I discuss savings and
retirement programs, corporate stocks and bonds, rental
real estate, mortgage lending, and a variety of other more or
less sophisticated methods for achieving wealth. My belief
is, provided with guidelines and encouragement, any
person can learn to master the techniques needed to become
prosperous.

However, I recently received a letter which took me
aback. Its writer, a woman from a small town in South
Dakota, forced me to reevaluate my presumptions when she
informed me: "My husband and I have read many of your
articles these past months and most of it sounds like good
advice, but we have a problem. Neither of us is confident
we can select good stocks, and we don't trust the mutual
fund salesmen. Neither do we want to own rental real

estate, hold mortgage loans, or do many of the other things you discuss. Our question is simply this: Can you provide us with just a few things we can do which require no particular knowledge or involvement, so we can retire in comfort when we're ready in about thirty years?"

Because I wasn't quite prepared with a ready answer, I set her letter aside . . . and there it sat for a couple of weeks while I mulled it over. What do I say to someone who hopes to achieve a comfortable retirement, but doesn't really want to do much of anything to bring it about?

I've given it some thought and believe I've figured it out. And while pondering the dilemma, it dawned on me a lot of other people must be of like mind. Devoting an adult lifetime adroitly acquiring assets goes against the grain for many persons. Whatever they attain in life comes with minimal expenditure of time and effort. To that end, I'll offer an approach, though it requires a caution: What I advocate will enable most persons to conclude their working years with enough to live in the style to which they're accustomed. But realize the standard of living achieved in this manner will be something less than bountiful. With this understood, let me describe three life habits to enable you to enter the retirement years with some degree of confidence.

1. Don't buy anything requiring you to pay interest. Whatever you purchase will be something you can afford. If you possess a credit card on which you charge things, pay the balance in full each month before the credit card company collects any interest. Operate this way and the interest rate on the card means nothing. If for any reason you can't conduct yourself in this fashion, cut up the card with a scissors. As another example of austerity, your dilapidated living room furniture is an embarrassment, with the only suitable furnishings beyond your budget. Your two likely solutions are to go into hock for months or years for the attractive set you want, or make do with low grade merchandise from a cheap discount house. A better decision is a choice friends of mine, a young couple, made many years ago. For three years their living room sat vacant until they could afford to furnish it with what they really wanted. As you might guess, they are today wealthy oldsters. Stepping out a little further, consider transportation. Your auto, though paid off, is now seven years old, with nearly 75,000 miles on the odometer, and no one you know drives anything this dated. A new car which can be purchased for $28,500 is available on a 5-year contract through a dealer at zero percent interest. Is this the way to go? Not on your life! Although you'll see no interest charged, it's there, built into the price of the car. Bought all cash, it would probably cost $23,000. So what do you do? You drive the old car until you can afford its replacement. And by "afford its replacement," whatever you acquire, new or used, will be purchased *cash on the barrelhead.* You do not borrow to buy consumer products—vehicles included. That's a recipe for a lifetime of poverty. As a final thought on the subject, if your friends think your auto has an old vintage look, consider it a compliment.

2. Own your residence free and clear. When your paycheck becomes a relic of the past, you'll want your housing costs to join it into oblivion. This means you own your home with no mortgage. It's easily accomplished. Early in your life purchase a house with whatever down payment you can afford. Choose a long-term, fixed-rate, fully amortized mortgage, and make the regular monthly payments until it's paid in full. As the years pass and your equity grows, avoid any temptation to dip into it for such things as schooling for the kids, the long-awaited vacation you've always wanted, or the surefire investment your brother-in-law guarantees will put you on Easy Street. Consider your residence a sacrosanct element of your retirement years, not to be further encumbered or compromised in any manner.

3. Set up your rainy day account. Regardless of however else you choose to spend your money over a lifetime, one thing must take precedence: As quickly as possible open a self-directed Individual Retirement Account (IRA). If you're married, filing jointly, with Adjusted Gross Income (AGI) less than $178,000, you're eligible for a particularly desirable Roth IRA. During each of your working years you and your spouse will each contribute the maximum allowable amounts into these accounts—$5,500 in 2013. They should be opened with a discount brokerage, online if you wish, into which will go interest-bearing vehicles as the sole holdings. These will be guilt-edge securities such as U.S. treasury notes and bonds, FDIC-insured certificates of deposits, money market accounts—with banks, not mutual funds—and perhaps high-grade short to medium-term corporate bonds, if you're willing to take the time to consider them. Admittedly, interest rates on such investments are at this time distressingly meager; I don't believe this will continue forever. The benefits you derive are twofold: You'll reap the rewards of compound interest and, under current rules the Roth IRA earnings will be entirely tax-free. If started early enough in life, such an account may well accumulate over a million dollars.

Let me sum it up. If you follow this three-point program I've just outlined, you'll enter your post-working years satisfactorily. Though you'll not retire in grand style, able to tour the world on your private yacht or bask in the limelight as a celebrated patron of the arts, at least you'll not be dependent upon family or government for your daily sustenance. It's an acceptable conclusion; most people in this world fare far worse.

31

PROCEED AT
YOUR OWN RISK

Beware of gratuities, for nothing
of value comes without a price.

Thanks to modern technology, we citizens are now offered far more opportunities to be taken advantage of than in the archaic past. A prime reason for this is *confrontation avoidance*: A hesitant swindler may be reluctant to confront a prospective victim face-to-face, but will do so readily if the pilferage can be performed remotely and anonymously. This is why the electronic media is such a danger; it helps the thief deal with those irritating inhibitions. What it does to naïve individuals inveigled into a scam is another matter.

With the increasing popularity of the Internet, there seems no limit to the types of chicanery perpetrated on the consumer. Simple theft and bunko schemes have been raised to new levels of sophistication, with virtually no lure too bizarre to find willing takers. As evidence of this, I've reproduced below an e-mail I recently received. You're viewing the message exactly as it arrived, with not one word altered. The alarming fact is this particular come-on, as crude as it is, actually induces persons to cooperate with the senders, thereby enabling the thieves to loot their bank accounts.

My dear,

Before I introduce myself, I wish to inform you that this letter is not a hoax mail and I urge you to treat it serious. I am a Director in Procurement Department with Petroleum Ministry here in Italy I obtained your email while searching for a reliable person, who could assist me in receiving transfer of a supposed contract awarded funds. This fund came as a result of over estimated contract awarded sums executed by foreign contractors in the Petroleum Ministry. The concerned Ministry has approved these over invoiced funds for payment.

The contracts which the over invoiced sums was created from has been executed and commissioned. What I am about to receive now, is the over estimated funds which was added during the process of obtaining the contracts for my own interest. This is a normal deal that goes in my Ministry by top officials.

On my part, all modalities have been worked out in ensuring a smooth conclusion of the contract payment to your bank account within the next few days. My department approves payments to contractors, and I happen to head the department. All I want from you is to receive these funds on my behalf as a Sub-Let Company, because as Government Official I cannot collect the funds directly from my Ministry, neither I am allowed by Law to operate/run foreign bank accounts. If you are trustworthy and can assist me in receiving the fund, do not hesitate to respond back to me immediately.

Please note that there is no risk involved in receiving the over estimated contract funds in your account. I want you to state in percentage what you shall have for participating in using your bank account to secure the funds. As soon as you indicate your interest, further details and the amount involved shall be given to you once I receive response from you. I hope I can trust you to treat this proposal with utmost confidentiality. My alternative email is [e-mail address provided]. Looking forward to hearing from you soonest.

Best regards,
Engineer [sender's name provided]

As implausible as the pitch may seem, it manages to convince a fair number of otherwise sane people to part with confidential information that results in their being robbed. Somehow a potent mixture of greed and gullibility acts to suppress the suspicions such a transparent ploy should have aroused. It's difficult to understand how anyone can be taken in by such a ruse, but it happens regularly.

As a guide for the unwary, I'd like to list the following Fraud Alert guidelines issued by the U.S. Federal Bureau of Investigation (FBI) as the most common danger signals by which scam artists seek to defraud the general public.

1. You receive a check for an item you sold on the Internet, such as a car, boat, jewelry, etc.

2. The amount of a check you receive on a sale is more than the item's selling price.

3. You receive a check via an overnight delivery service.

4. You receive a check connected to communicating with someone by e-mail.

5. A check is drawn on a business or individual account different from the person buying your item or product.

6. You're informed you are the winner of a lottery that you did not enter.

7. You are instructed to either "wire," "send," or "ship" money, as soon as possible, to a large U.S. city or to another country such as Canada, England, or Nigeria.

8. You've been asked to pay money to receive a deposit from another country such as those in the preceding example.

9. You're receiving pay or a commission for facilitating money transfers through your account.

10. You responded to an e-mail requesting you to confirm, update, or provide your account information.

I'll conclude this lecture with a few general observations. The number and variety of people seeking to take advantage of the public are limitless. Your best defense against predators will be a well-honed skeptical approach. Recognize that in this hostile world, strangers rarely befriend other strangers out of the kindness of their heart. And above all, keep one truism always in mind: If someone offers to conspire with you to defraud a third party, understand *you* are the actual mark.

32

MONEY AND HEALTH—THE INSEPARABLE LINK

The finest in health services
is everyone's birthright—
no matter who must pay for it.

Benjamin Franklin neatly summed up life's three most valued qualities when he wrote "Early to bed and early to rise, makes a man healthy, wealthy, and wise." Not only do the factors—*health, wealth,* and *wisdom*—constitute the basis of a satisfying life, but they depend upon one another. It's obvious that engaging in drug abuse results in wealth impairment. But perhaps equally telling, if you fail to control your monetary affairs, it will reflect on your well-being. A recognized cause of depression and accompanying physical maladies is financial distress. The term for this sort of illness is *psychosomatic.* It follows: If you handle your money imprudently, plan to be sick.

A concluding word on Franklin: Although his emphasis on health, wealth, and wisdom makes sense, I'm not so sure about his *early to bed and early to rise* advice concerning longevity, for Ben, who died at 84, couldn't match song-writer Irving Berlin, composer of *Oh how I Hate to Get Up in the Morning*, who made it to 101.

Let's acknowledge up front, as with many other aspects of living, part of good health is pure luck. Nothing much can be done to prevent certain birth defects and congenital conditions. Also various ailments occur which are unpredictable and incurable, at least at the present state of medical technology. So it's no overstatement that the prime responsibility of each thinking person is to pursue practices to maximize the term and quality of life. Unfortunately this is more easily said than done. In this hostile world, there is an array of special interests thriving on the reality or illusion of bad health, and with this we must deal.

Our first consideration in the quest for well-being relates to how our bodies react to what we ingest and the activities in which we engage—or *fail* to engage. One of the more heavily promoted businesses in America is the diet industry. The desire to be thin constitutes a national obsession, with no limit to the books, articles, and programs promoting weight loss. Bookstore shelves are filled with such titles as *Eat More, Weigh Less Diet* and *Eat, Fast & Stay Slim*. The most sought-after female fashion models are clearly skeletal, and the eating disorders of anorexia and bulimia are common, with sufferers frequently featured on TV talk shows in all their emaciated horror. Despite this, a study conducted in the past decade by the National Center for Health Statistics revealed for the first time, over half of all Americans can be classified as overweight, with extreme obesity increasingly common. The cause of this widespread dietary schizophrenia is a complex matter and far beyond the scope of this book. All I'll present here are sensible suggestions that work.

Consumption of food—the intake of calories—is only half the equation. Bodily activity—the burning of those calories—is the other half, the two as inexorably related as *yin* and *yang*. Attendant to these are individual factors such as appetite, metabolic rate, and physical limitations. The goal for each of us: to optimize our bodily appearance and function over a lifetime in a prudent manner. That, of course, requires development of reasonably sustainable eating and exercise habits. More specifically, any program requiring abnormal effort over a prolonged period of time will fail. The clear significance: "Diets" *do not* work. So the obvious question becomes: "What, if anything, *does* work?" You are in luck, because something does indeed work.

Over the years my reading included such best sellers as *The Drinking Man's Diet, Dr. Atkin's New Diet Revolution*, and *The Beverly Hills Diet*, to mention just a few. Some of the books and articles contain a strain of reasonableness, while in others the recommendations are literally off the wall. Of them all, one author was clearly ahead of his time. That man, the late Nathan Pritikin, truly revolutionized the world's thinking with his *Live Longer Now*, first published in 1973. Eventually the medical community came to accept his concept of a regimen high in complex carbohydrates while low in fats, sugars, salt, and caffeine. Although the book is now out of print, a more recent work, *The Pritikin Program for Diet & Exercise* is available. It lays out a program which can promote a long and healthy tenure on this earth.

The second half of the quest for health involves a commitment to physical activity. As expected, there is no limit to the number of books and articles offering the ultimate exercise program, with each title suggesting its own view of nirvana. If you are not intrigued with *Stretch Yourself for Health & Fitness*, perhaps *The Superstar Workout* will suit you better. Then again, *Hanging Out: The Upside Down Exercise Book* may strike your fancy, unless a critical time shortage drives you instead to *Thirty Days to a Beautiful Body*. As with books on diet, some of the exercise programs seem reasonable, others make little or no sense and more than a few are potentially dangerous. And while on the subject of danger, be aware many persons in the physical fitness business, particularly health club counselors and high school physical education instructors, are sadly out of their element.

So again the question: Is there a guide on physical fitness by any author in which you may place confidence? This surely is your lucky day. The book is there to be found. The author is Kenneth H. Cooper, M.D., and the approach outlined in his book, *The Aerobics Program for Total Well-Being*, formed the basis of the Royal Canadian Air Force exercise program. The essence of his method is selection by the participant of one or more exercises of choice, wherein the benefit of each activity can be assessed by an easily measured point system. Dr. Cooper's concept is a technique to encourage life-long activity. It is as close to *must* reading as you will find.

I'm sure it comes as no surprise both Pritikin and Cooper are an integral part of my life. Together they enable me to maintain my college graduation weight of 154 pounds while enjoying tasty and filling quantities of grains, pasta, rice, and potatoes. Furthermore, a five times weekly routine of light weights and swimming, together with a weekly hike in the hills, makes stairs easier to climb, prolonged periods of work less taxing, and a noticeable absence of aches or pains. Although physical ailments come my way, as inevitably they must, I manage to keep them from becoming debilitating while maintaining an easily carryable weight along with usable muscles and an efficient circulatory system. Although each of us will eventually conclude our visit to this small planet, the time we spend here will be far more sustainable if we treat ourselves as though the warranty expired.

In connection with your physical activity, I'll make a few specific suggestions. It pays to engage regularly in more than a single exercise. There will be times when you experience discomfort of one sort or another. When that happens, cease the particular activity which seems to cause the problem. Above all do not "work through" the ailment, regardless of any contrary advice. When your body is telling you something, pay attention! It knows what it's talking about.

Another rule to follow: warm up before, and warm down after, each exercise routine. My swim begins slowly with the regular pace and stroke not reached until the seventh or eighth lap. Again, the last half dozen laps are like the beginning. This may seem unduly cautious, but it pays off. Over the years I encountered other swimmers who became friendly but competitive pacing partners. I often felt the temptation to get an early lead, but resisted it. As a result of insufficient warm-ups, more than one of these friends eventually sustained permanent injuries which ended their swimming.

The final suggestion relates to what can best be described as *resolve*. A successful exercise program requires participation no less than three times weekly, year after year. For this sort of commitment, many of you need to include all the positive reinforcement you can get. Convenience is important. If you must travel long distances or endure unpleasant surroundings, you make excuses to drop out. Some people find a treadmill or stationary bicycle set up at home in front of the television to be the best inducement. My preference is a club where workouts can be shared with other like-minded enthusiasts. The habit of meeting in a congenial atmosphere with the same people day after day works as a draw, so much so that a factor in the choice of a building site for my present home included proximity to the club. Nonetheless, what works for you is the determining factor.

There's not a whole lot more to add. You know what you must do. It's your job to do it. However, I'll leave you with the following bit of verse which may—or may not—further encourage your resolve.

♦   ♦   ♦

WORKING OUT

When gathered with the other sports
  His countenance would shine.
Adorned in red and yellow shorts,
  He cut a figure fine.

His jersey top and peaked cap
  Were trimmed in royal blue.
With canteen on his shoulder-strap,
  And Nike sneakers too.

He hit the trail with gaited trot,
  Where he had run before.
A bramble bush, now long forgot,
  Was what he stumbled o'er.

Back on his feet and through a field,
  He hit the barbed wire chain,
But luckily the blood congealed . . .
  He hardly felt the pain.

The gravel road he dashed atop,
  Revealed his healthy glow.
You'd hardly think the ten foot drop
  Would wrench his ankles so.

A bulldog then took up the chase,
  It's hard to say just why.
Although it couldn't keep the pace,
  It gnawed him on the thigh.

Along the highway next he sped,
  The traffic closing in.
Exhaust fumes thick about his head,
  And tar burns on his shin.

At last upon the river bank,
  In sight of home, you see,
In seven feet of mud he sank,
  But somehow wiggled free.

A tattered mess, he staggered back,
  A vision to astound.
Appearing like a gunny sack,
  He crumpled to the ground.

When asked by friends to tell them, please,
  What should they make of it?
"It's just that I have . . . koff . . .
                  gasp . . .
                    wheeze . . .
  Been jogging to stay fit."

33

AN INVESTMENT LESSON

*The secret of success in virtually
every endeavor is mastery of the details.*

Back in the spring of 1974 a three-line ad in the classified section of the *Los Angeles Times* caught my eye. It offered an attractive return on short-term loans secured by houses in Orange County, California. Having purchased and serviced real estate loans for years, it seemed worth looking into. I found something unexpected.

Behind a stained gray metal desk in a room no larger than 12' X 12' on the second floor of an old frame office building in Anaheim, sat a small man in his mid-30s. He claimed to be a real estate broker and explained he planned to purchase, renovate and resell homes from troubled owners for a profit. He admitted having neither money nor credit, so needed to arrange private financing for his program to work. He suggested we look at a house a couple of miles away and drove over in his aging pickup truck.

I saw a typical 3-bedroom tract house, about ten years old, in need of paint, cleaning, carpets, and yard work. Its likely value of about $125,000 when fixed up, and an existing 6% FHA loan of $80,000, made it attractive. The broker suggested $15,000 cash to the seller with a take-over of the existing loan. He asked me to make a six-month, second mortgage loan of $20,000 to him as purchaser, enough he said for the seller, rehab, holding and sales costs. He offered to pay interest of 2% per month, which represented 24% per annum.

I saw both good and bad. On the plus side: a favorable FHA loan at a fair rate of interest—the less onerous the senior loan, the less risk to the junior lender. The offer of a high rate of return and a short holding period also seemed attractive. Furthermore the loans totaled no more than 65% of the property value. But no positive comes without a negative. The first defect: a 24% usurious return—unenforceable regardless of the willingness of the borrower to pay it. The second problem: an uneasy feeling of this character sitting on the other side of the desk. The owner of the property controls all aspects, including renovation, marketing and servicing the mortgages. What is my position? A casual observer entitled to foreclose if not paid. As proposed, this sort of involvement constituted high risk.

Another way existed to resolve both objections. Instead of my providing money for his purchase at a specific interest rate, I proposed to pay the seller the $15,000, take title to the property in my name, and deliver $5,000 to the broker. The mortgage becomes mine to service and I give the broker a six-month option to purchase at $110,000. By this arrangement he need only renovate and resell within the anticipated six months for his profit. The change for me was vital in that it eliminated the dual problems of usury and control. He accepted my proposal and we formalized the agreement a few days later.

He moved speedily, putting the house in showable shape within a month, finding an acceptable buyer for $125,000 two weeks later, and closing escrow in another five weeks. Within less than three months he made $13,700 with no cash outlay—certainly a handsome profit. In this same 3-month period I pocketed $8,600. We both did well.

A second house became available within a month and a third followed shortly thereafter, both renovated with sales pending in escrow by late September. I remember my visit to the broker's office to sign the last of the documents. Things had changed considerably. His offices, containing perhaps a dozen employees, now occupied about two thousand square feet in a modern building on a fashionable boulevard. But most dramatic of all was the huge polished walnut desk behind which he sat, along with an exceptionally attractive secretary at a smaller desk nearby. While conducting our business I thought of a movie from long ago: *Will Success Spoil Rock Hunter?* Though generally satisfied, my feeling of discomfort returned.

In mid-October we entered into agreements on another house. By late November, with no progress reports, and phone calls to his office unanswered, I became concerned. My investigation that weekend told the story. I found his offices locked and the business obviously shut down. Visits to the house later in the day literally required my forcing entrance.

Over the next two months my wife and I personally renovated and marketed the house. Luckily the real estate market held and we suffered no actual cash loss, though compensation for our efforts was probably below the statutory minimum wage rate.

Although this may sound like the end of the story, there's a bit more you should know, as well as a few warnings I'll pass on. To begin with, the broker ran into problems as his expenditures rapidly exceeded his income. Why he felt the urge to expand and luxuriate as he did only a psychiatrist can tell, but it certainly led to his undoing. Personality disorders often cause people to cut corners, and he cut more than a few, which included absconding with trust money from other investors. In due course he served two years in State prison.

There are two other points of note. First, recognize the importance of dealing from a position of strength. Were the initial investment made as a real estate loan, my only recourse would have been foreclosure under the mortgage. Possession of the property might have taken a year and resulted in a washout. But with ownership of the house in my name from the onset, I needed only aggressively commandeer. That made the difference between profit and loss. In short, security is crucial.

The other matter concerns uneasy feelings. There are times you perceive something is wrong but cannot put your finger on it. Don't dismiss these sensations. They may be the most accurate part of an analysis, and at the least, signal danger. Pay attention to these vibrations.

On a humorous note, you may be amused at how the broker managed to buy properties so cheaply. If nothing else, it shows a talent at connivery. He first searched the tax records for houses with out-of-state owners. He then drove by each property. When he found a vacant house, he quickly decorated the front with items of debris he carried in the back of his pickup truck, including a couple of large inner tubes which he hung near the front door. After taking a Poloroid picture of his creation, he piled the junk back into the truck, returned to his office, and mailed the photo along with a letter to the owner, suggesting a buyer might be available. Though it achieved the desired result, I don't suggest anyone emulate his method.

34

"SIT STILL
AND BEHAVE
YOURSELF!"

*Never do anything that public opinion
or your own sense of right do not approve.
Hire someone else to do it.*

Though it goes back a lot of years, I remember my childhood. I qualified as a "high strung" youngster. I specifically recall my principal mode of foot travel by age four: full gallop. And when seated, my hands and feet moved constantly. Whatever deficiencies I exhibited did not include a lack of energy. And I tend to recollect, in conjunction with the gyrations, my thoughts joined into the action. I'm certain many of the sensations which passed through my head during those years reflected my tempo. Naturally, growing up exuberantly in those years insured full occupation for my mother, for when I ran, she ran close behind. Though I don't recall the instance, I'm told that I once bolted across Chicago's Lake Shore Drive during rush hour, only to be pulled to safety within inches of a fast moving taxi. Luckily I avoided serious mishaps during those *hyperactive* years. Thereafter, as I entered adolescence, my bodily functions naturally slowed down, and I'll concede now, after many decades, everything is much slower, indeed.

Gazing back in retrospect, it occurs other children displayed a similar zest for activity, dictating a common parental admonition of the day: "Sit still and behave yourself." Since many of my friends and classmates acted, to a greater or lesser degree, as did I, we must conclude these traits are not unique. This, then, leads me to a revelation. Profitable moneymaking operations impress me, and I'm particularly intrigued when an innovative approach is employed. Well, I've considered various possibilities and think I've come up with a winner. Picture this, if you will. Suppose we establish ourselves in the child counseling business and are able to sell the idea that children who exhibit such characteristics as finger tapping, whistling, scratching or stretching, fidgeting, displaying high energy levels, and exhibiting boredom in the classroom, are seriously disturbed and need our services. You see, by simply defining many childhood traits as a *disorder*, we create a mass of customers who need our services. The opportunities are truly exciting. With a concerted effort, which includes the coining of an impressive name for the ailment, then lobbying the government to fund its treatment through such programs as the Americans with Disabilities Act, and finally establishing a prestigious national association of practitioners to treat the afflicted, there is no limit to the possibilities. There must be millions of youngsters, particularly boys, who display those symptoms. If we can swing it, each child will require our counseling right through puberty.

Hmm, it just occurred, if we hope to pull to off this charade, we'll need to enlist the support of the nation's mental health practitioners. Our contention that bright and active children are somehow seriously maladjusted will need to be corroborated by some prestigious organization. Let's see, who might we approach to *anoint* our project? By George, I've got it! What better groups might we get to back up our claims than the American Psychiatric Association and the American Psychological Association? As both will benefit financially from countless hours of counseling to be sold, they should be willing to throw in with us.

Oh, oh! I've just spotted a fly in the ointment. A distinct drawback in treating this spurious ailment will be actually demonstrating some behavior modification. What shall we do? Ah ha, I think I've figured how it can be arranged. We'll need a medication to suppress normal childhood traits, and I know of one that will work well. It's methyl-α-phenyl-2-piperi-dineeacetate hydrochloride, known commercially as Ritalin. An oral dose of 50 mg lasts about 4 hours, so we'll prescribe it four times daily. With any luck, the overall quantities required will be immense, so we're certain to get a favorable endorsement from the pharmaceutical industry. Though it causes a few inconvenient side effects such as appetite suppression and insomnia, we can overcome this problem by simply administering a sleeping pill at bedtime. I'll concede there may be a few imponderables in all this. I'm not sure what long-term effects there may be in keeping a child perpetually drugged during the developing years. To put things in context, another medication somewhat akin to Ritalin, Eli Lilly's Strattera, at one time drew the attention of the Food and Drug Administration by its possible suicide inducing propensity. Nonetheless, if the potential profits for the drug companies are sufficient, they'll likely find a way to assure the public their product is safe. Possibly they can arrange tests demonstrating no evidence of any sort of risk. If that approach doesn't quite swing it, then perhaps in compliance with FDA guidelines they can announce a black-box warning will be added to the drug's label. As no one except a tort lawyer reads those labels anyway, almost everyone ought to be satisfied.

Yes, indeed, I'm elated with the fine program I've devised. I can't see any disadvantages at all—well, at least none I'm willing to discuss. However, you know what they say: To make an omelet you've gotta break a few eggs. Of course, I'm glad no one dreamed up a program like this when I was a kid. What with my high energy, I'd have been one of its victims for sure. After a half-dozen or more years counseled to act abnormally, while being pumped full of God knows what, there's no way to predict the resultant brain scrabbling. Under such circumstances, growing up becomes a nightmare, and there's no way to know what the final adult product will be . . . but maybe this is just something we'd better not mention.

35

WHERE CHARITY BEGINS

Few persons in the charity business
really give a rap about charity.

As you're aware, this book is devoted to the subject of money. And since that's what you expect, I'll not disappoint you . . . well, not exactly, though I must warn you this time I'll not dwell on making money, but, rather, on its disposal. I want to discuss giving it away. If you're asking why I advocate *giving it away*, the reason is simple. In the final analysis, there's a practical limit on personal consumption, beyond which satisfaction is marginal. At some point in our finite lives there must be more than mere acquisition. In this world you'll find deserving people, and the opportunity to share your bounty in a meaningful way is exactly that—an opportunity. There's satisfaction in giving back a portion of your good fortune, and this is the place I've chosen to discuss it. Fair enough for a reason, I hope.

Before I get into the details of generosity, I want to pass on a few observations concerning America's charitable foundations. The more than one million philanthropic organizations that solicit grants and donations, and which presumably exist to bestow beneficence as provided in their charters, function in a strange sphere of unreality. Of the more than three hundred billion in public donations these organizations annually receive, a huge portion of the funds never see their way to any intended purpose. As to applicable rules, federal law provides private foundations need donate no more than five percent of their assets each year to retain their non-profit status. Add to this the provision that administrative expenses such as salaries and rents may be included in this five percent and the results are predictable. The actual philanthropy of many foundations is abysmal.

This leads to the question: What eventually happens to these massive unspent amounts? Anyone with an understanding of mankind knows exactly what happens.

> *Human nature is such that insider abuses of any organizational system are, and always have been, integral to the system, not aberrations from it.*

Very simply, those who control the operation tend to pass benefits on to themselves and their cohorts.

A few statistics will give you an idea of how it works. In a recent year, the average giving by 26 major foundations, each worth $1 billion or more, amounted to 4.7 percent of assets. To put *giving* in perspective, expenses and overhead were included in this category. But the real puzzle was determining how the assets were used. In that year the directors of the 20 wealthiest private foundations each received more than $400,000, even as the value of their investments sagged. Add then the practice of nonprofit organizations to provide their senior officials with elegant accommodations, plentiful benefits, and loans often subsequently forgiven—in emulation of for-profit corporations—and the picture begins to come through clearly.

You might ask whether there's some way of distinguishing the good charities from those not-so-good. Within certain limits, yes. Statistical data, mostly based on the IRS Forms 990 filed annually by all non-faith-based charities earning more than $25,000, is available. However meaningful evaluation often requires reading between the lines—a tough job if you don't know what to look for. In getting down to fundamentals, I believe in ensuring the ultimate recipient is both *deserving* and *identified*. This, of course, rules out many charities as it's difficult to know what happens to the huge sums which annually disappear into such organizations. I'll have a bit more to say on this subject near the end of this book, so stay tuned.

So where do we go from here? My belief is charity begins at home . . . though not with the cynicism normally intended. There's another way to target your donations. Let me suggest how this might be done. Imagine for a moment that you're an architect with a love for your profession. What better gift might you make than to enable young engineering and architectural students to pursue that career? You can establish a private non-profit educational foundation into which you will contribute sums of money. These funds will become available for scholarships to students chosen by the foundation directors whom you select, perhaps faculty members at a nearby college. Selections will normally be made in May at the end of each academic year. The students will receive payments, say on a monthly basis, while pursuing their degrees at a university as long as they continue to perform satisfactorily, and it will be your task to monitor their performance. Not only do deserving students benefit directly to the extent of nearly 100 percent of your contributions, but your donations to the foundation qualify as deductions on your tax return.

Instead of concluding this subject with nothing more than a vague exhortation, I want to provide something more tangible. Specifically, the following is the actual Policy Statement, complete with details, of my private foundation, in operation since the 1980s. Those of you who wish may use this as a guideline for establishing and operating your own foundation. And good luck to you.

◆　　◆　　◆

POLICY STATEMENT FOR SCIENCE SCHOLARSHIP FOUNDATION

If America is to continue to thrive in a competitive and increasingly technological world, it must encourage its more talented citizens to strive for achievement in the physical sciences.

The Science Scholarship Foundation functions to provide scholarships to students who have demonstrated a high degree of academic proficiency in the physical sciences at the community college level, and who desire to pursue a course of study leading to a bachelor's degree in chemistry, chemical engineering or biochemistry.

The Trustees of the Foundation raise funds through solicitation of donations from private citizens, organizations and businesses, and the general public, as well as by other means. The funds thus raised are distributed by the Trustees to the scholarship-recipients periodically during the school year. It is anticipated that the distribution amounts, which may vary from time to time at the discretion of the Trustees, will be sufficient to enable each scholarship-recipient to subsist, as nearly as possible, without the necessity of outside employment and, thereby, permit the student to devote his or her full time and attention to the course of study.

Selection of scholarship-recipients is made by an independent Board of Selection; the members are appointed by and serve at the pleasure of the Trustees, and are comprised of college professors within the community college system. The Board of Selection evaluates applicants and awards scholarships on behalf of the Foundation, subject only to availability of funds and in compliance with the general guidelines established by the Trustees. These general guidelines require that to be selected, the student:

1. Be a citizen of the United States.

2. Not be a relative or any Trustee or Member of the Board of Selection.

3. Will have completed those chemistry couses known at Saddleback Community College as 1A, 1B, 12A and 12B (or equivalent courses at other schools) and attain a grade point average of not less than 3.5 in these four courses.

4. Will have completed the necessary physics and mathematics courses required for a chemistry, chemical engineering or biochemistry major.

5. Obtain the approval of the members of the Board of Selection.

6. Enroll as a chemistry, chemical engineering or biochemistry major in and attend on a full time basis a college or university which teaches an approved

curriculum, and maintain a scholastic record at such institution which is satisfactory to the Board of Selection as a condition to continued receipt of scholarship funds.

7. Meet any other requirements established by the Board of Selection which are not inconsistent with the stated intent of the Foundation.

It is the specific intent of the Trustees that, in the award of scholarships, there shall be no discrimination of any sort by reason of race, creed, religion, national origin, age, sex or marital status. Additionally, it is not the intent of the Trustees to predicate a scholarship award upon a student's financial need, and the Board of Selection is free to give whatever consideration to this factor that it feels is consistent with the Foundation's stated intent.

It is expected that the Board of Selection will maintain a complete set of records in connection with its functions. These records should include all applications accepted, minutes of meetings held, evaluation summaries of all applicants (both successful and unsuccessful), and any other documents which may be pertinent to the selection process. These records, which shall be the exclusive property of the Board of Selection, shall be available to the Trustees upon their request.

In summary, the policies under which this Foundation operates have been designed to help encourage talented students to select chemistry, chemical engineering or biochemistry as their major field of study. It is to this end that the Trustees will continuously monitor the operation over the coming years and make such modifications to the program as may appear necessary and proper for its improvement.

36

HOW TO COPE WITH THE INCREASED COST OF DYING

"The time had come that comes to all."
Richard H. Dana, Jr.

An interesting and somewhat alarming article appeared in my local newspaper awhile back. Its title, "Make death a part of the cost of living," caught my attention. The author, Ric Edelman, a prominent financial advisor and host of the weekly *Ric Edelman Show*, pointed out the average expense for a funeral in the United States is now about $10,000. He then described how costs for necessary items such as casket, embalming, hearse, flowers, cemetery plot, headstone, and a myriad of other services, can be controlled and minimized. He concluded with a recommendation to contact the Funeral Consumer Alliance, an organization in service since 1963, for referral to a local nonprofit Memorial Society.

Mr. Edelman's advice is sound. There's no valid reason why a death in a family need involve a financial burden to the survivors. And make no mistake: A *financial burden* is exactly what many a death becomes, for the societal pressures brought to bear on the next of kin are often formidable. Understand, the funeral industry in America is as aggressively marketed as any consumer product you will find. One of the most striking depictions of the callous mortician is found in Edwin O'Connor's outstanding 1956 political novel *The Last Hurrah*, later made into a movie starring Spencer Tracy. However, in the late Jessica Mitford's *The American Way of Death*, published in 1963, the practices of that business received thorough and accurate documentation. Regardless of your feelings concerning Miss Mitford's Communist affiliations, the book became an important factor in subsequent legislation which attempted to curtail the many abuses then existing. Thanks to those laws, and to a more rational attitude by a segment of the population as to proper disposal of last remains, the bereaved today enjoy a somewhat better chance to avoid victimization. Nonetheless, do not presume the business is all sweetness and light. A funeral home's typical 300 to 500 percent markup on casket prices makes your friendly used car salesman seem almost philanthropic by comparison. But what's particularly onerous is while negotiating for an infrequently used product, the bewildered customer with a 96-hour interval between the death and the burial cannot easily say: "I'll think it over a while and let you know."

This seems an appropriate time to reveal my personal attitude concerning treatment of the deceased. To begin with, many deaths are not a tragedy, but rather the welcome conclusion of a long-tenured and pleasant life. To quote the late syndicated newsman Paul Harvey: "There ain't no use worrying; you'll never get out of here alive." With this understood, it's only reasonable we all plan for our eventual demise to insure minimal trauma for those we leave behind. Most importantly, the actual disposition of the body should not cause uncertainty and/or financial hardship. It's a simple matter to make arrangements long before age and illness intervene to create urgency. For many years, my wife and I have been members of the *Tri-County Memorial Funeral Society.* An initial cost of $5 each entitled us to register with an affiliate mortuary, Pierce Brothers of Anaheim in our case. Our instructions are on record that upon death, our remains be cremated at once and the ashes disposed of in the simplest and least elaborate method. As recently as autumn 2011, such arrangements required one 30-minute visit to the funeral home, with total cost for these services, including all necessary certificates and taxes, $772.32. I'm pleased to report, despite inflationary pressures on such items as gasoline, groceries, and university tuition, the cost to perform this vital disposal function remains essentially unchanged. Thanks to the Internet, it's easy to locate a facility which will offer a cremation service that's simple, dignified, affordable, and ecologically responsible. One such firm is City Funeral Service of Yonkers, NY, www.nycremation.com, which quotes a price of $625. Another is Funeral Depot, a nationwide enterprise, www.funeraldepot.com, whose charge is $795. These are but two examples; there are many more throughout the country.

It naturally goes without saying, the concept of an inexpensive and unadorned disposition of last remains goes against the grain for many persons. Promoted over the centuries by powerful nationalistic, religious, and commercial interests, society learned to embrace the ritualistic funeral, at which it became fashionable to display the decorated cadaver. The concept that final internment of a corpse must take place amidst a ceremony to rival a royal coronation became universal. This is an attitude defying logic. If any sanity is to return, it's particularly important to separate the disposal of the body from any final tribute to the deceased. In reality, they have nothing to do with one another, despite an established agenda by the funeral industry to tie them together into an emotional package so to milk the ceremonies for all they're worth. It's my firm belief any desired memorial services be performed at least a week following final disposition of the remains. Above all, entertain no recommendations from the funeral director except as to bare legal requirements for disposal of the body.

A concluding thought is in order. At the time of death—whether anticipated or not—the next of kin may not be the best person to oversee the funeral. It might be wise to relegate decisions involving these arrangements to someone with less emotional involvement, be it a business associate or more distant family member. Remember always, true respect and compassion for the deceased is reflected by the relationships sustained during life, not by the hysterics which take place following death.

37

FIVE FRIVOLOUS ITEMS THAT ARE REALLY WORTH IT

The three necessary ingredients for an enjoyable life:
1) Something meaningful to do
2) Friends with whom to share your experiences
3) Something intriguing to look forward to

For the past many years I've written articles extolling the virtues of thrift, outlining programs for sensible spending, and presenting guidelines for sound investment. Perhaps, then, you'll understand why I found myself taken aback recently by an e-mail that said: "You talk a lot in your content about the smart and practical things to do with money. However, when people do come into money, they are going to 'blow' some of it. So would you share some ideas on which items are a smarter choice when it comes to frivolous spending, or admittedly unnecessary luxury things just to make people feel good?"

I'll confess I drew a momentary blank. Quoting from William Jennings Bryan's testimony in the 1925 Scopes evolution trial: "I don't think about things I don't think about." Well, I've since thought about it; perhaps the five extravagances I've listed below are justifiable. But first a disclaimer: The thought of "blowing" money—any money—doesn't sit well with me. However, I suppose I can tolerate seeing up to ten percent of a windfall spent frivolously, though even *that* causes me to cringe a bit. You may now read on.

1. You've just received an unexpected tax refund of $6,500 and want to celebrate your *good fortune*, even though it was your own money before you overpaid the IRS. How might one-tenth, or $650, be enjoyably spent? Why not take a weekend vacation as my wife and I did recently? We chose Palm Desert, an easy drive from our home. Two night's accommodation at Residence Inn by Marriott at $215 per night, dining at our favorite restaurants, an afternoon spent at Palm Desert Tennis Club, and an evening stroll through the shops along El Paseo after dinner, left us still in possession of a portion of that pre-allocated $650. We returned home relaxed and refreshed. There are certainly worse ways to spend your dollars.

2. Aunt Hilda just passed on at the ripe age of ninety-three, leaving you—her favorite grandniece—$15,000. After carefully stashing $13,500 of it into your money market account (which I'm sorry to say is still paying only peanuts), you might choose to indulge yourself with the rest. So where can you spend $1,500 to good advantage? Why not get rid of that old 27" television set you've stared at for the past fourteen years and begin viewing your favorite shows in somewhat grander style? A visit to Best Buy Stores reveals you can purchase a 37-inch Samsung HDTV with HDMI Interface and Built-in Stereo Speakers for $1,330. Added tax, delivery, and installation charges still place the set in your home at less than the

target figure. And with any luck, you'll continue to enjoy your acquisition for fourteen more years.

3. Though it seems like antiquity, common stock in Berkshire Hathaway 'A' once commanded three hundred dollars per share, and the five shares you had the good fortune to acquire just sold for a cool $850,000. After setting aside enough to pay state and federal capital gains taxes, you're still $650,000 ahead. Perhaps you deserve a treat, and why not the toy you've always wanted: a classic or vintage automobile to reveal your devotion to the motoring world of yesteryear? One of the more popular vehicles fitting this bill is the Model A Ford, built between 1928 and 1932. Whether you select a nicely conditioned '28 Roadster convertible with rumble seat for $22,900 or a fully restored '31 Tudor sedan at $21,000, you'll garner attention as you cruise your neighborhood streets. Add to that a membership in one of the Model A clubs across the country and you'll meet fellow-enthusiasts with whom you can share your fervor. As an alternative for those of you who are understandably concerned over the maintenance demands of an aged auto, here's further thought. There are now firms manufacturing factory replicas using all modern mechanical parts, but which appear to be originals. They're easily repairable and attractively priced. A '30 Phaeton convertible sedan replica can be purchased for $15,500.

4. You expected it never to happen. Amidst somewhat mixed feelings, you're now a retiree. Included among the mixed blessings are two benefits: a final retirement bonus of $25,000 and the prospect of free time you've never before experienced. What better way might you begin those leisure years than with an ocean voyage? A multitude of fine luxury cruises are available at surprisingly reasonable prices. During seven days in an

ocean view cabin on Holland America Lines' *MS Oosterdam*, at only $659 per person double occupancy, you'll depart and return San Diego, visiting the Mexican ports of Cabo San Lucas, Mazatlan, and Puerto Vallarta. If the Caribbean Sea is more to your liking, Celebrity Cruises' *Century* out of Fort Lauderdale, Florida, with similar accommodations, offers a 7-day excursion to Montego Bay, Grand Cayman, Cozumel, and Costa Maya, at $650. A somewhat more exotic 7-day cruise aboard Peter Hughes two-masted sailing vessel, *Komodo Dancer*, out of Bali, visits several South Sea Islands. Its ocean-view cabin prices begin at $1,605. Depending on the time and *prudently-disposal* money available to you, there's virtually nowhere on earth not accessible.

5. My final suggestion for cash disposal may not qualify as *frivolous*, but it can prove personally satisfying. Your local high schools and community colleges regularly recognize exemplary students with commendations, often accompanied by monetary awards. The funds normally come from citizens in the community, where each donor designates the academic discipline to be recognized. Presentations are customarily made at formal school awards ceremonies, and offer incalculable encouragement to awardees. Amounts to recipients can be large or small. I've seen donor grants as modest as $50 as well as multiple scholarships exceeding $50,000. So, if you regard education as important, and desire to spur students to greater achievement, simply contact the school of your choice and let them know of your willingness to participate.

38

25 SIGNS SHOWING YOU CAN HANDLE MONEY

Any program which seeks to confer lasting benefit upon a person without placing a heavy premium on individual achievement must fail.

The ability to master your money is not something that just happens. It takes time, training, and temperament. Nonetheless, there are those among us who have figured out how it all works, and what it takes to prosper.

Are you one of those persons who managed somehow to get the hang of it? If you recognize yourself in most of the twenty-five following scenarios, then you can confidently answer "yes" to that question.

1. Your credit card bill is paid in full each month with never a penny in interest incurred.

2. You understand the variable annuity in which your neighbor just invested will prove to be a sad mistake.

3. Despite orchestrated furor by the media, you recognize the $40 it costs to fill your vehicle's gas tank is cheaper in today's dollar than the $20 it cost 20 years ago.

4. You enjoy financial talk shows for their entertainment value while knowing 95% of what's said is nonsense.

5. The only type of life insurance you'd ever consider purchasing is a term policy.

6. You're not tempted to invest in something because of a hot tip you get from a friend or relative.

7. You have serious doubts the 3-unit course in basic English composition offered at Eleganté University for $900 is any better than a similar course conducted at Midtown Community College for $60.

8. You're sufficiently sophisticated in real estate to know the worst house in the best neighborhood beats the best house in the worst neighborhood.

9. You owe nothing on the vehicle you drive.

10. You have a pretty good idea by mid-November how much your income tax obligation for the current year will be.

11. When hearing the S&P 500 Index just hit an all-time high, you're not inclined to call your broker with a buy order.

12. It's beyond your comprehension why anyone not certifiably insane purchases a *timeshare* property.

13. Your checking account balance never drops below the minimum limit that triggers a monthly service charge.

14. You're aware an option to pay your auto insurance premium in two installments, with a "modest convenience fee" instead of a single payment, probably works out as a loan at about a 25% interest rate.

15. Although you thoroughly enjoy the home in which you live, it's considerably less expensive than you can afford.

16. You know practically nothing about the option market—and intend to keep it that way.

17. You feel instinctively every dollar you contribute in FICA taxes to the Social Security system is a dollar lost to you forever.

18. Whenever you're negotiating a purchase and qualify to receive a discount, you do not hesitate to ask for it.

19. You entertain no illusions a financial advisor will provide sound counsel merely because of the Certified Financial Planner (CFP) designation held.

20. You make the maximum possible contribution to your retirement funds.

21. Whether your choice of lipstick is the $20 Chanel selection from Macy's, the $5.46 Max Factor brand from Osco Drug, or the 94¢ Wet 'n Wild tube from Target, you recognize the essential ingredients are the same.

22. You find it baffling why anyone buys a lottery ticket.

23. You cannot remember when you last borrowed money for an unexpected emergency.

24. The newspaper advertisement offering a half-pound silver commemorative medallion from *The Perfidious Mint*, at the "special advance price of only 249 dollars," forces you to suppress a laugh.

25. You exhibit no confidence in the concept of "Investor Confidence."

If the sentiments expressed in most of those situations do not reflect your thinking, you're not in control of your financial destiny. In this case, you can use a little guidance. A visit to the *Newsletter Archives* on my website at www.onthemoneytrail.com might be a good place to start.

39

A VIEW FROM
THE FAR SIDE

In church and in state it is rule or be ruled;
In courtship and marriage it is fool or be fooled;
In logic and law it is nick or be nicked;
In gambling or trade it is trick or be tricked;
In treaty or war it is beat or be beaten;
In the struggle of life it is eat or be eaten.

— Anon

Those of you who follow my articles regularly are accustomed to advice on how to make money . . . or on how to save it . . . or how to invest it. By diligently absorbing the suggestions I've given over the past years, you possess the blueprint needed to pursue the *prosperous life*. If you simply follow the guidelines, display ordinary intelligence and are not exceptionally unlucky, you most assuredly will become successful—*wealthy*, if you prefer that word. Whether or not this will fulfill your ambitions or even make you contented is another matter. But if nothing else, one indisputable benefit of wealth is the luxury of avoiding many of the people you find distasteful, be it an overbearing boss, a difficult client, or an offensive co-worker. Despite the reality that financial independence is not nirvana, the old adage is accurate: Success may not be *everything*, but failure isn't *anything*.

There is one matter of importance I've largely ignored until now, and it relates to the burdens and obligations of success. Consider an undisputable truism: *Your stature is measured by the way you handle success.* Whether you like it or not, wealth brings with it certain demands and responsibilities, and if you ignore them you will regret it. As you become wealthy—*recognizably* wealthy—certain aspects of your life change, and not all for the better. Although the problems of meeting the mortgage and financing the children's schooling may no longer exist, other problems move in to take their place. Your relationship with friends and relatives begin to change as you are viewed as something apart. It seems that admiration and envy are opposite sides of the same coin, and as your perceived fortune grows, you will be the recipient of both emotions. Your advice and assistance will be solicited, and although you may at first welcome the attention as a novelty, you will eventually find it more burdensome than complimentary. Regardless of your contribution, it often provides no satisfaction to the recipient, and *you* will be held to blame for the failure. Irrespective of your intentions, for every bouquet, expect to receive at least one brickbat. In this regard I've become convinced over the years that it's better to be rich and not look it than to be rich and have it obvious to everyone.

An even more significant effect of prosperity can be your relationship with yourself. Despite the personal unpleasantness of failure, it imposes no demands on the ego. Success is another matter entirely, and the pressures it creates can be formidable. It's fulfilling the mundane requirements needed to meet daily financial obligations that keeps many people in balance. When this necessity is removed, the balance often goes with it. If you then add to that the ability to acquire unneeded possessions, exert unwanted influence on others, and seek unwarranted involvement, the potential for impairment can be unlimited. Whether or not these pressures in any way caused the untimely deaths of such celebrities as film director and actor Andrew Koenig or musician and songwriter Mark Linkous is uncertain, but obviously financial success did not prevent them. Ultimately you must come to terms with whatever success you enjoy. Perhaps if it comes slowly, you acclimate more easily. Quite likely the most difficult task of all is for it to be dumped on you precipitously—so in deference to your next of kin, give some serious considerations to that when it comes to writing your will.

At this point, I've about run out of preachments. There's only so much extolling and cajoling possible before the audience *turns off, tunes out, and drops dead*, as the late counter-culturist Timothy Leary might have declared. However, out of consideration to those of you who are yet unconvinced by anything I've said, I'm prepared to offer you a path to prosperity wherein you're not required to know anything or do anything. The following lines of verse describe the one surefire method, so seize it if you can.

◆   ◆   ◆

SUCCESS STORY

Y' wanna' know how I done it?
As simple as A – B – C.
It took real guts when I come here,
A'way back in '63.

I didn't get very much schoolin',
Dat seemed a waste of time.
'N the jobs I had . . . all krappy . . .
Jus' too much dirt 'n grime.

But I stuck it out 'til now, yuh see,
Who knows where things kin lead?
I figgered somethin' good would break,
Damned sure I could succeed.

They ain't no one kin tell me dat
I didn't pay my dues.
T' prove it I'm retirin' wid
A million smackeroos.

I guess I otta' menshun',
In case yuh wanna know,
Aunt Madge just kicked da' bucket . . .
Dat's where I got da' dough.

Business & Economics/Personal Finance

Are you likely to prosper in life?

This book can make the difference. It was written . . .

- Not by a banker, who merely stores other peoples' money.

- Not by a financial advisor, who merely fantasizes about other peoples' money.

- Not by a stockbroker, who merely places other peoples' money.

- Not by an economist, who merely philosophizes about other peoples' money.

This insightful author, an entrepreneur who long ago achieved prosperity, shares his knowledge and experience. The revelations disclosed will empower the reader to deal with the world in a more realistic manner and employ the tools and techniques this book describes.

The Road to Prosperity embodies the heart of the author's ten years of newsletters, written monthly under the heading *On the Money Trail*. Those articles directed attention toward financial matters, normally with an emphasis on personal achievement in a variety of endeavors. The newsletters received wide attention and distribution, being prominently displayed in numerous publications, both in print and online. They regularly appeared in *Families Online Magazine, Producers Web, Dr. Laura, Healthy Wealthy –n Wise, The Sideroad, Family Corner, Money Solutions, Education World,* and many others.

ABOUT THE AUTHOR—Al Jacobs has been an entrepreneur for nearly a half-century. His business experience ranges from investment in real estate, mortgage loans and securities to property management, appraisal, civil engineering, and the operation of a private trust company. An advocate of lifelong learning, he has completed innumerable professional courses including accounting, law, insurance and taxation. He lives in the coastal community of Monarch Beach in Orange County, California, in a home of his design, with his wife of fifty years.

DANA PUBLISHING
P.O. BOX 3143
DANA POINT, CA 92629

ISBN 9780986050008

90000 >

9 780986 050008